GW01339053

ec

Best wishes
from all
at Investec

Dublin
Simon
Community

Specialist Banking | Asset Management | Wealth & Investment

Investec Bank plc (Irish Branch) is authorised by the Prudential Regulation Authority in the United Kingdom and is regulated by the Central Bank of Ireland for conduct of business rules. Investec Capital & Investments (Ireland) Limited trading as Investec Wealth & Investment and Investec is regulated by the Central Bank of Ireland. A member of the Irish Stock Exchange and the London Stock Exchange. Calls may be recorded.

Strokestown and the Great Irish Famine

This book was designed and typeset by Anú Design for
Four Courts Press, 7 Malpas Street, Dublin 8, Ireland
www.fourcourtspress.ie
and in North America for
Four Courts Press
c/o ISBS, 920 N.E. 58th Avenue, Suite 300, Portland, OR 97213.

© Ciarán Reilly and Four Courts Press 2014

A catalogue record for this title
is available from the British Library.

ISBN 978-1-84682-555-2 hbk
ISBN 978-1-84682-554-5 pbk

SPECIAL ACKNOWLEDGMENT
The author and publisher would like to thank
Investec for their generous support.

All rights reserved. No part of this publication may be reproduced,
stored in or introduced into a retrieval system, or transmitted, in any form or by any means
(electronic, mechanical, photocopying, recording or otherwise), without the
prior written permission of both the copyright owner and publisher of this book.

*'Thank you for the care lavished here
on such a wonderful part of our heritage.'*

President Mary McAleese commenting on the Strokestown Park House
Archive on the occasion of the launch of the OPW/Maynooth University
Archive and Research Centre, 13 November 2008.

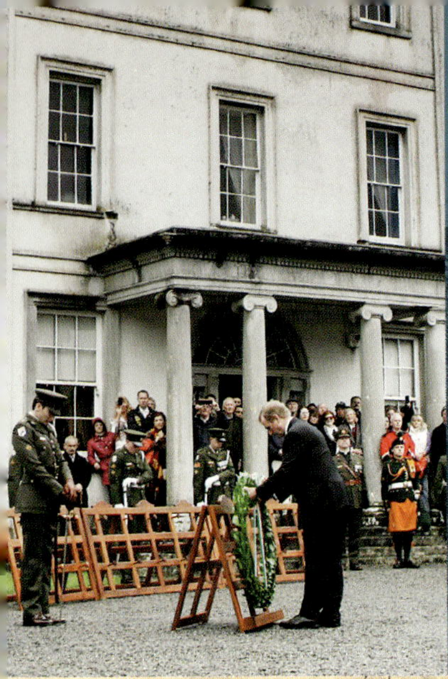

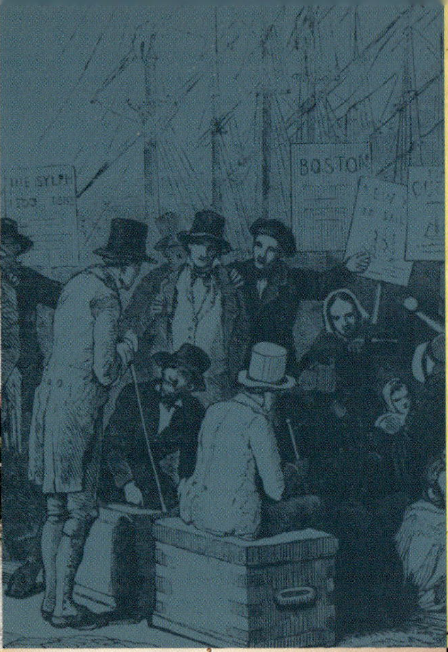

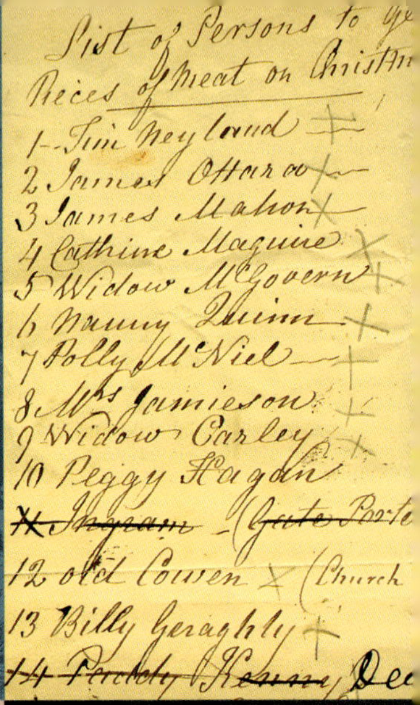

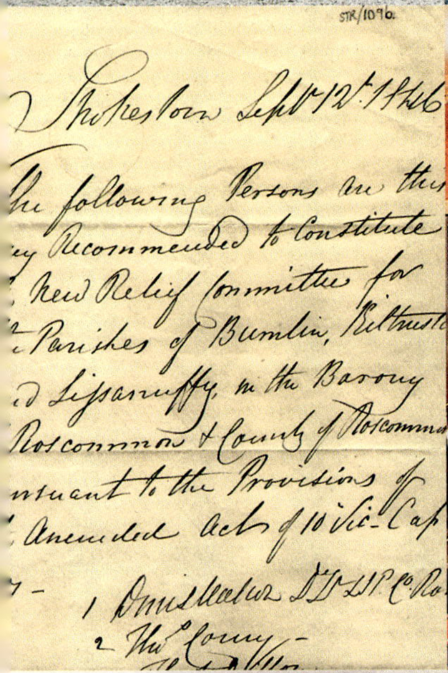

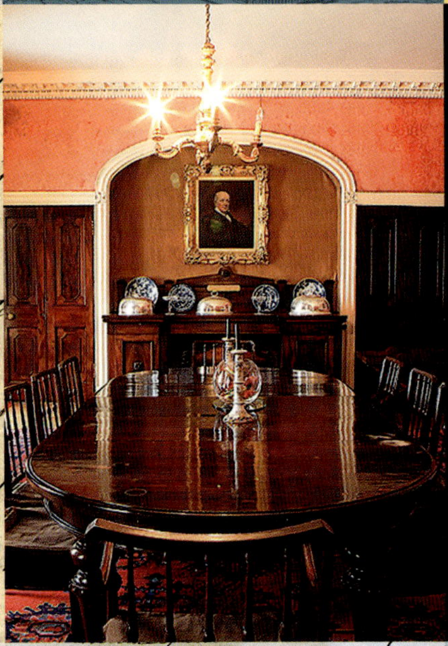

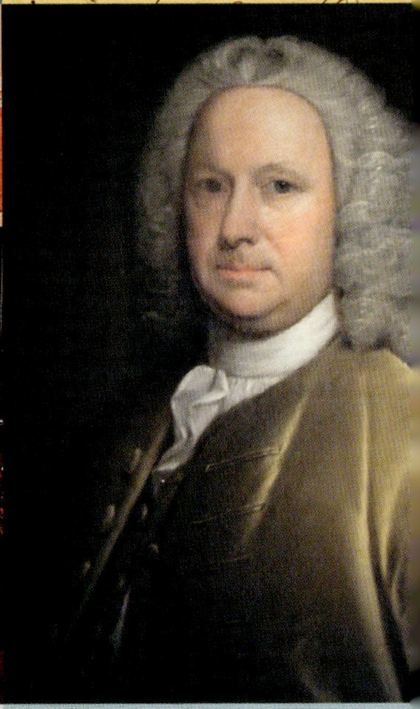

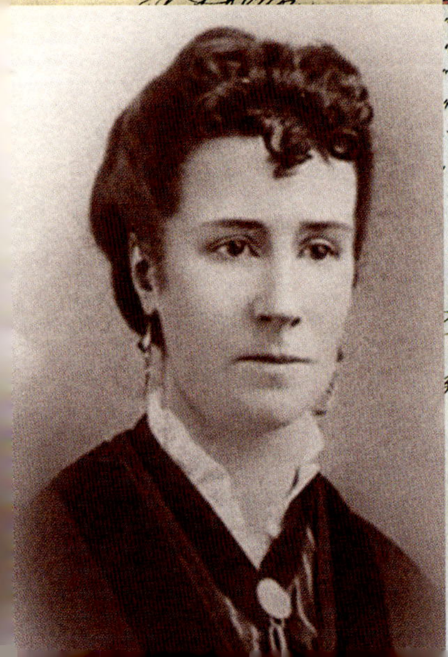

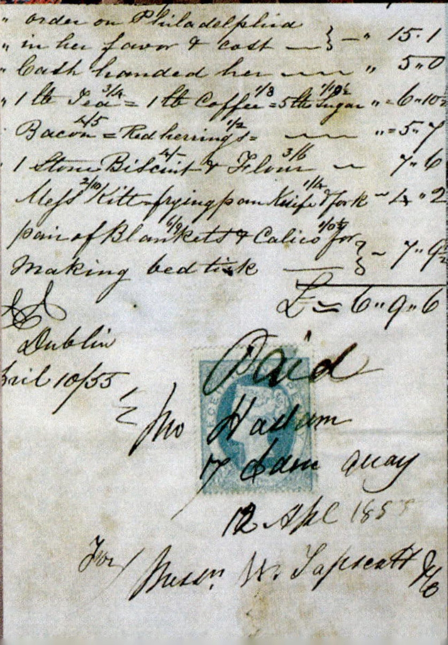

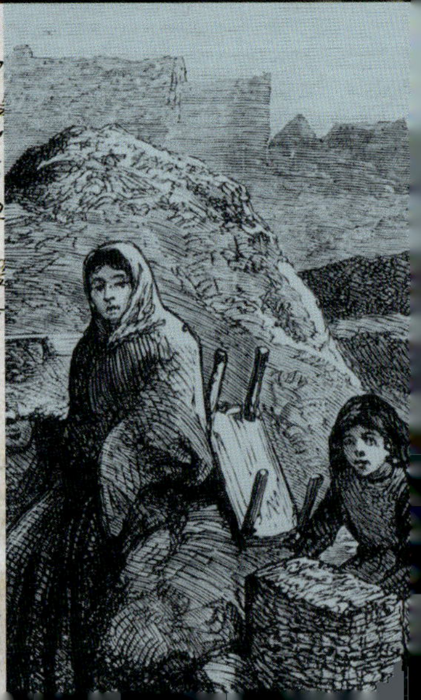

Contents

	List of abbreviations	viii
	Foreword by Mary McAleese	ix
	Acknowledgments	xi
	Glossary	xiv
	Introduction	1
1	'Towards the abyss': Strokestown on the eve of the Famine	11
2	'The poorest peasantry on the face of the earth': Early relief efforts, 1846–7	33
3	'Destitution prevails on this country': changing attitudes on the Mahon estate	49
4	'Orphaned to the world': assisted emigration in practice	65
5	Targeting the 'snug' tenantry: prelude to murder	79
6	'Worse than Cromwell and yet he lives': the murder of Major Mahon	91
7	'With renewed vigour': the clearances continued	111
8	The exodus continues	133
9	Recovery and renewal: post-Famine Strokestown	147
10	Conclusion: social memory and culpability	163
	Postscript: the making of the Irish National Famine Museum	179
	Notes	189
	Bibliography	207
	Illustration credits	210
	Index	211

Abbreviations

CSHIHE	Centre for the Study of Historic Irish Houses and Estates
FJ	*Freeman's Journal*
GML	Guinness & Mahon Letter books
NAI	National Archives of Ireland
NLI	National Library of Ireland
OPW	Office of Public Works
PM	Pakenham Mahon
PRONI	Public Record Office of Northern Ireland
RJ	*Roscommon Journal*
RLFC	Relief Commission papers
SOCP	State of the Country Papers
SPHA	Strokestown Park House Archive

Foreword

This book aims to introduce the reader to the Strokestown archive and to provide an insight into the varied experiences of Famine gleaned from the records of those who inhabited the Strokestown estate in the 1840s. The archive is one of the largest collections of Famine documents in the world. Illuminating the text and providing the reader with a unique insight into Famine Ireland, most of these documents have not seen the light of day since they were generated almost 170 years ago. Although the 1990s (and later) witnessed an outpouring of scholarly work on the Great Famine to commemorate the sesquicentenary, only a handful of studies examined the impact of the Famine on individual landed estates. As Terence Dooley has argued, estate records can reveal 'the reality of estate life as opposed to the myth which has often been handed down in oral history or, indeed, in biased history texts'. This is particularly true of Strokestown's records.

A particular strength of the book is the insight it provides into the plight of the landless labourers and the cottier class, providing a voice for the people who have been long absent from the narrative of the Famine. These were the classes worst affected by the catastrophe that befell Ireland in the 1840s. From the hundreds of petitions sent seeking help from the landlord we see the trials and tribulations that the Famine brought. It is significant that the vast majority of these were written by women, many of whom had been abandoned by their husbands and families. This book is the most in-depth study of the effects of the Famine on a landed estate and its community. Roscommon suffered a devastating population decline during the period 1841 to 1851, yet we know little of how the Famine impacted on individual lives.

Much of the population decline was the result of emigration; as many as 5,000 people emigrated from the Strokestown area alone during the Famine. Of these, some 1,490 people were part of the assisted emigration scheme of 1847. This book traces the progress of these emigrants in the New World and highlights some remarkable

Glossary

abatement: in the early years of the Famine, landlords and their agents granted reductions or 'abatements' in the rent to alleviate tenants who had been affected by the loss of the potato crop.

arrears: a legal term for part of a debt, i.e., rent that is overdue.

assisted emigration: during the course of the Famine more than 80,000 people were 'assisted' in emigrating, meaning that their landlord paid for their passage.

Board of Guardians: when the Irish Poor Law Act was introduced in 1838 a Board of Guardians was elected to run the affairs of the workhouses within each designated area. By 1851 over 150 workhouses had been built in Ireland.

combinations: as distress grew in the early 1840s tenants came together forming 'combinations' against the payment of rent. Often these concerted efforts were enough to force the hand of an agent/landlord.

conacre: a system whereby land was rented on an 'eleven-month' basis, with the contract renewed from year to year. It was a preferred method of renting land among many landlords as it gave the tenant no legal entitlement to the holding.

cottiers: a class of people who generally owned little more than a half acre of land.

demesne: the 'Big House' was usually surrounded by a demesne or designed landscape enclosed by a wall. The entrance or approach to a demesne usually included a gate house.

'gale'/'hanging gale': most tenants were given a period of grace, usually six months, to pay their rent, which usually fell due half yearly on 1 May and 1 November. This was known as the 'hanging gale'.

Gregory/ 'quarter acre' Act: introduced in 1848, it stipulated that holders of more than a quarter of an acre of land could not be deemed destitute and thus were not entitled to relief. It resulted in thousands of impoverished cottiers surrendering their land to landlords in order to obtain relief.

jointures: the monetary provision for a wife after the death of her husband, which was paid by the estate.

middlemen: men who rented land from a landlord and in turn sublet the land, often at a higher price.

Molly Maguires: a secret oath-bound agrarian society that operated in the nineteenth century, who agitated on issues such as taxes, tithes and rents.

Orangemen: members of the Orange Order or the Loyal Orange Institution, a body founded in 1795 to uphold the rights of Protestants. They were named in honour of William of Orange, who defeated the Jacobite forces at the Battle of the Boyne in 1690. The 12th of July is the annual celebration of William's victory at the Boyne.

Poor Law Act: introduced for Ireland in 1838, it allowed for a system to supply relief to the poor. It was based on the English model, which had been introduced in 1834.

Poor Rates: these were charged on every person residing within a local electoral division for the maintenance of the workhouse. Landlords were required to pay the Poor Rate for those with a holding valued at under £4, and, as the Famine progressed, many landlords decided to clear these tenants from their estates.

Repealer: a follower of Daniel O'Connell's Loyal National Repeal Association, who sought to overturn the 1800 Act of Union between Britain and Ireland.

subdivision: a favoured method of land division in pre-Famine Irish society whereby land was divided into smaller pieces.

tithes: an annual payment of one-tenth of produce paid to the Established Church. They were greatly resented by all denominations.

turbary: a right to cut turf.

under-tenants: those who rented land from a middleman/large farmer.

watchers: these were employed to provide information to the land agent or landlord about the activities of tenants on their estate.

workhouse: a place where the poor and destitute could find accommodation and shelter in return for carrying out basic duties. Conditions of entry into the workhouse were strict and it was seen as the last resort of the destitute.

Strokestown Park House was constructed in the mid-1690s, and reflected the rising fortunes of the Mahon family. Built on the site of an earlier castle belonging to the O'Conor Roe sept, much of the house was reputedly redesigned in the 1730s by the German-born architect, Richard Castle.

Having purchased Strokestown House in 1979 from Olive Hales Pakenham Mahon (1894-1982), extensive renovation work was carried out before the house was officially opened to the public in 1987.

Introduction

In the shadow of the 'Big House', Ireland's first Famine museum was established at Strokestown in 1994. From the outset, Strokestown's owner, Jim Callery, saw the museum as a means of balancing the history of the 'Big House' by using the original estate documents detailing the lives of the tenantry during the Great Famine to tell the story of Ireland's greatest social catastrophe. After Strokestown House was purchased in 1979 from Olive Hales Pakenham Mahon (1894–1981), extensive renovation work was carried out before it was officially opened to the public in 1987. At the time many people felt that it would have been better if Callery had razed the house and destroyed its voluminous archive, closing a chapter of history that they did not want to revisit:

> The attitude was to wipe them [country houses] off the face of the earth. There would be as little left of them as there was of the poor cottiers who were wiped out in the Famine and after it.[1]

These feelings, as the historian Terence Dooley has noted, were 'not lost on those who subsequently established the Famine Museum at Strokestown'.[2] Granted the

When the Westward Group purchased Strokestown Park in 1979, Jim Callery stumbled upon the 'Cloonahee petition' of August 1846. This document related to the townland where Callery was born, and he realized that the archive had a public story to tell. His plans for Strokestown were thereafter altered.

distribution rights to Scania products in the Republic of Ireland in 1976, Jim Callery required additional lands to expand his business, Westward Garage. Although relations with Olive Pakenham Mahon had not always been amicable, she encouraged Callery to bid for Strokestown House and demesne, which was put to public auction in 1979. Jim Callery's offer was accepted, but he allowed Mrs Pakenham Mahon to remain in the house until 1981. It was during his first visit to the house when he examined the archive room that Callery's intentions for Strokestown House were altered. Stumbling upon the 'Cloonahee petition', dated August 1846, this document from the townland where he was born, and still lives, struck a chord. Part of the petition read:

> Our families are really and truly suffering in our presence and we cannot much longer withstand their cries for food. We have no food for them, our potatoes are rotten and we have no grain.[3]

According to Christopher Ridgway 'he [Callery] realized he had stumbled upon a cache of enormously important documents that had a public story to tell'.[4]

The Strokestown Park House Archive is one of the most extensive estate collections in Ireland, comprising over 50,000 documents, including rentals, accounts, correspondence, maps and plans, property deeds, rent books, labour returns, pamphlets, press cuttings and photographs.[5] Of particular importance are the papers relating to the Great Irish Famine. Given the paucity of Famine records in many other estate collections, the Strokestown archive has thus an added significance because of the microcosmic insight it offers into the Famine at estate and local level.[6] Following discussion between the board of Strokestown Park House and the Centre for the Study of Historic Irish Houses and Estates, Maynooth University, it was decided that the papers should be loaned for preservation and cataloguing purposes to the OPW/Maynooth University Archive and Research Centre at Castletown. This research centre, officially opened in November 2008 by then-President of Ireland, Mary McAleese, was established to facilitate the care and study of archives and other sources dealing with the history of Irish estates, their houses and inhabitants. It also facilitates research in the decorative arts.[7] Since 2008 the archive has undergone extensive conservation work, while cataloguing is ongoing in the hope that the collection will be made accessible to the public in the near future.[8] Speaking at the launch of the research centre, President McAleese commented that the Strokestown archive was:

> a national resource, a national treasure trove. With this special archive we will be able to interrogate the past more deeply ... the deposit of the Strokestown Park House papers at this new research centre will continue to shed light on the history and suffering of the Famine and connect this generation to the forgotten people of the past.[9]

Besides years of mismanagement, a decline in the livelihood of the vast majority of the Mahon tenants meant that on the eve of the Famine most were in arrears; some had not paid rent in up to five years. Inheriting the estate in 1845, Major Denis Mahon found that debts amounted to more than £30,000, as this account book for the year 1843 shows.

Twice a year the Strokestown tenants were expected to present themselves at the estate office to pay their rent.

When the Famine struck in 1845 Major Denis Mahon was charged with providing relief for the teeming population on his estate. Among the thousands who were relieved daily throughout 1846 was Mary Lenehan of Elphin Street, Strokestown (number 15 on the list), an ancestor of former President of Ireland, Mary McAleese.

The archive informs on the economic, social, political and cultural life of Roscommon in the mid-nineteenth century, ranging from the occupants of the 'Big House', to middlemen and large farmers, to the cottiers and landless labourers. This latter group – the cottiers and landless labourers – have largely been denied a voice in the Famine narrative. However, their voices are the most numerous in the Strokestown archive. The documents shed light on more than 10,000 people who experienced famine at first-hand and who were witness to hunger, eviction, emigration and death.[10]

This book is based on what is perhaps the most important famine archive to have survived. It is a comprehensive analysis of what happened on one estate – Strokestown

Pre-Famine Ireland

In the pre-Famine period, Ireland underwent a massive population explosion. Between 1770 and 1841 the population rose from two million to over eight million people. This was due largely to the shift to widespread tillage production, bolstered by the European wars of 1792–1815, when Irish farmers and landowners secured high prices for provisions. In addition, cottage industries, primarily based on linen and wool, provided extra income for Irish families. All of this was to change dramatically after the defeat of Napoleon in 1815, when the Irish economy went into decline. With much of the land of Ireland let to middlemen on long and favourable leases, tenants and sub-tenants had been allowed to subdivide the land, with disastrous consequences. Holdings were too small for viable farming. With almost half of the population dependent on the potato, by the early 1840s poverty was endemic and efforts to promote agricultural improvement had largely failed. In 1838 the British government introduced the Irish Poor Law Act, which made provision for the establishment of the workhouse system as a means of alleviating poverty. The workhouse, modelled on the English system, was not designed for times of famine. Built to accommodate about 600 'inmates', when the Famine struck more than three times that number were huddled in individual workhouses.

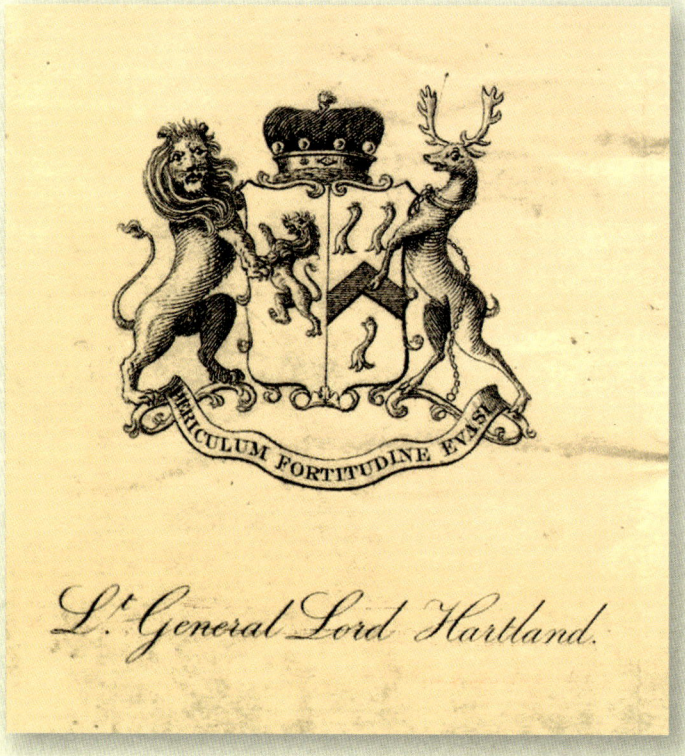

(*Top*) The Gothic entrance to Strokestown was built in the 1790s, linking the town with the 'Big House', but most tenants would never venture beyond its gates. (*Left*) For his support for the passing of the Act of Union in 1800, Maurice Mahon was elevated to the peerage as Baron Hartland.

8   STROKESTOWN AND THE GREAT IRISH FAMINE

– offering new and original insights into how the Famine played itself out at a local level. The book examines controversial estate management policies that led to the eviction and emigration of thousands of tenants and the murder of the landlord who was responsible.[11] It also examines the culpability of the local community; in other words who benefited from the plight of the under-privileged tenants. In the social memory of the Great Famine at Strokestown, the assisted emigration of 1,490 people to Canada, the murder of Major Denis Mahon there in 1847 and the subsequent clearance of as many as 3,000 tenants from the estate in the years 1848 to 1851, predominates. While it is certainly true that the emigration schemes and the clearances caused considerable unrest and this may have contributed to the murder of Major Denis Mahon, this is not the whole story. The Strokestown Famine archive highlights the fact that there are still major questions to be answered in relation to the greatest social calamity in modern Irish history.[12] For example, how widespread and effective were local efforts to alleviate the plight of the impoverished? How did the local community react to the clearance of thousands of people? Who benefited from these clearances? How did those who emigrated fare in their receiving communities? Was there a dislocation of country house life during the Famine or did it continue relatively unaffected?

Opened to the public in 1987, Strokestown Park is home to the Irish National Famine Museum, established in 1994.

Strokestown Park House was greatly altered in the early nineteenth century.

Travel writers in Ireland were renowned for their flattering descriptions of the towns and villages associated with the landed ge largely because the landed gentry were the patrons of many of their publicatio

1

'Towards the Abyss': Strokestown on the Eve of the Famine

> Strokestown is delightfully situated in a charming glen under Slievebane [sic] mountain — This is a good market and post town, watered by a beautiful river, situated in a sporting and eligible country, and which produces the best tillage in this county.[1]

Travel writers in Ireland were renowned for their flattering descriptions of the towns and villages associated with the landed gentry, largely because the landed gentry were the patrons of many of their publications.[2] The pseudonymous Skeffington Gibbon (his real name was Augustus O'Kelly) was one such writer who praised the Mahon family, residing in Strokestown, county Roscommon, indicating that they were 'charitable and good natured to their domestics and tenantry'. These sentiments were reiterated by others throughout the early nineteenth century including Samuel Lewis, who described the Mahon estate as 'unrivalled in beauty and fertility'.[3]

Such descriptions often did not reflect reality, and nowhere was this more true than at Strokestown. A sharp decline in the Irish economy, caused by the ending of the Napoleonic Wars in 1815, coupled with a demographic explosion, resulted in gross overcrowding, rising poverty and crime throughout Ireland. Tenants who had once survived by supplementing their income with cottage industries were

(*Top*) Photograph of the main street in Strokestown, with the estate house in the background, *c.* 1950s. (*Left*) Thomas Mahon (1701–82), known as 'Father of the House of Commons', was responsible for Strokestown being developed into the model estate town that we see today. It was his ambition for it to have the widest street in Europe, which he modelled on the Ringstrasse in Vienna.

pushed further into poverty, and this led to increased social discontent, violence and crime. Much of this unrest was generated by the immense push for access to land, which would come to define events in Roscommon during the Famine. The public perception of the landed gentry, particularly at Strokestown, differed greatly from that presented by Gibbon or Lewis. Reflecting the public dislike of the Mahon family, the antiquarian John O'Donovan wrote in 1838 that 'no man of talent has hitherto appeared among them' and poked fun at the fact that 'a young man called Neherny has more influence locally' than any of the Mahons.[4]

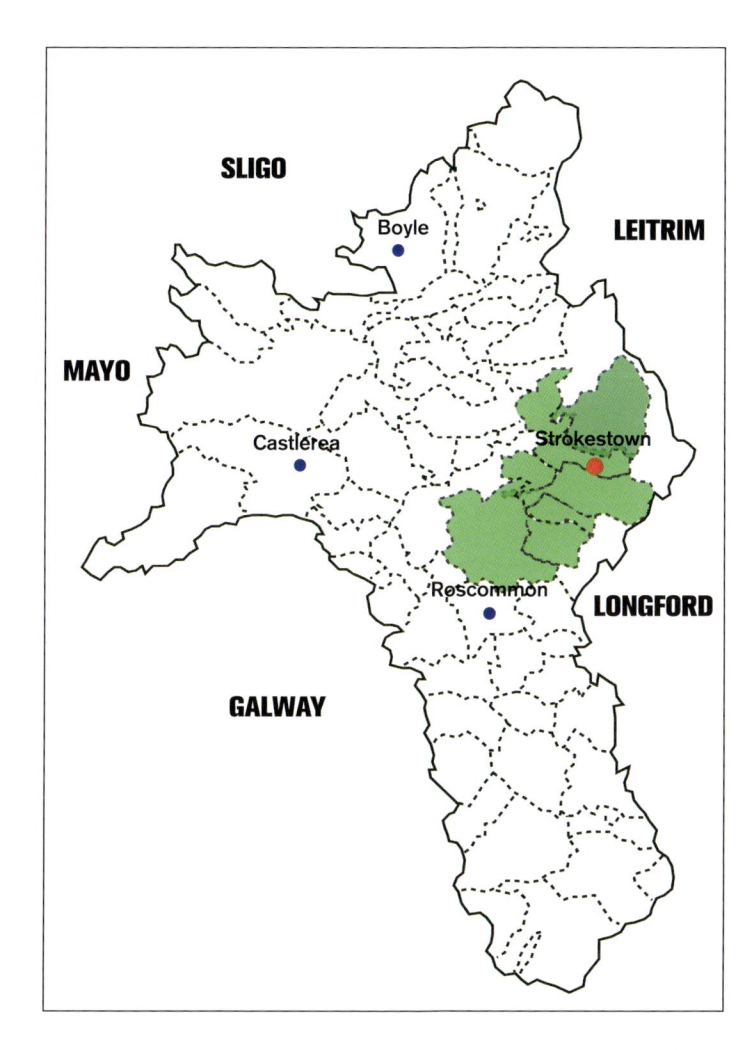

Centred on the town of Strokestown, by the early eighteenth century the Mahon estate amounted to over 11,000 acres.

Strokestown is located in east Roscommon close to the county boundaries with Longford and Leitrim. The relatively low-lying landscape is punctuated by Sliabh Bawn (named after the fairy queen, Bagna), which reaches a height of 262 metres. On the eve of the Famine the Sliabh Bawn area was among the most densely populated in Ireland, described as 'teeming' with paupers.[5] Until the mid-seventeenth century the area around Strokestown belonged to the O'Conor Roe sept, before it was granted to the Mahon family in the 1650s, although some confusion exists as to the precise nature of the grant.[6] Prior to his arrival in Strokestown, Nicholas Mahon (1620–80) owned land in Elphin and Aughrim, while documentary evidence from 1662 suggests that he purchased Strokestown from Edmund Dillon. By contrast, local lore suggests that the family first arrived in the area having been rewarded for their services in

> **LORD CHANCELLOR.**
>
> The 21st day of August, 1838.
>
> In the matter of
> MAURICE, LORD HARTLAND,
> a Lunatic.
>
> WHEREAS John Mahon, Esquire, Receiver in this matter, this day petitioned The Right Honorable the Lord High Chancellor of Ireland, setting forth and stating as in said Petitioner's said petition is stated; and praying His Lordship to order, that it be referred to Thomas Goold, Esquire, the Master, to inquire and report whether it would be for the benefit of said Lunatic, and his estate, that any, and what, proceedings should be adopted by said Petitioner against said several Tenants, to restrain them from cutting said turf, for the purpose of selling same; and burning the said lands. And if the said Master shall find that proceedings should be instituted for that purpose, that said Petitioner might be at liberty to proceed from time to time pursuant to said report, and without further order, against the Tenants of said estate, who now, or may hereafter, cut the turf of said lands for the purpose aforesaid, or burn or destroy the surface of the lands in their possession; or for such other order as to His Lordship might seem meet. Whereupon and on reading the affidavit of Denis Mahon, Esquire, the Committee of the estate of the said Lunatic, filed the third day of August instant, It is ORDERED, by His Lordship, that the said Tenants of the Townland of Currys, in the petition and affidavit mentioned, be respectively restrained from cutting the said turf-bog of the said townland, for the purpose of sale, or otherwise than for their own consumption: and that the said Peter Keary, tenant to part of the lands of Lavally, and John Ganly and William Higgins, tenants to part of the said lands of Farnmore, part of the estate of the said Lunatic, and all persons acting or deriving under them, be restrained from turning up and burning the surface of the said lands, unless cause, within ten days after service of this Order upon the said Tenants of the said townland of Currys, and upon the said Peter Keary, John Ganly and William Higgins, herein before named, good cause shall be shewn to the contrary.
>
> **DAN. M'KAY, C. C.**

In 1836, before a *Commission de lunatico inquirendo*, Revd Maurice Mahon was declared a lunatic and the estate vested in the Court of Chancery. There followed several years of neglect in the management of the estate, which greatly affected an already impoverished tenantry.

the army of Oliver Cromwell, and indeed according to Gibbon, it was the English Puritan who 'threw [Strokestown] into the possession of the Mahon family'.[7] Largely because of what was to follow during the Great Famine, the Mahon [later Pakenham Mahon] family endeavoured at all opportunities to portray a Gaelic ancestry stretching back to Brian Boru.[8] An interesting account of the Mahon lineage is provided in the correspondence of Thomas Mahon (1766–1835), 2nd Baron Hartland, who argued that the family was 'of great antiquity and had originated in county Cork' where Castle Bernard, near Bandon, was once known as Castle Mahon. Hartland also noted that the elder brother of Brian Boru, Mahon, was king of Munster for sixteen years, and that several times the family married into the O'Brien's, earls of Inchiquin.[9] This Gaelic past was again cited at the coming-of-age address of Nicholas Hales Pakenham Mahon (1926–2012) in 1947, as proof of the family's connection to the local community.[10] Susan Hood has suggested, however, that this may not be the case, and it is more likely that

FORMULA

REQUESTED TO BE FILLED UP FOR MR. BURKE'S

PEERAGE AND BARONETAGE.

Name in full.	The Revd Maurice Mahon, is unable to [manage] his affairs from paralysis, he resides at Strokestown House with the Guardian of his Person and Property Denis Mahon Esqr
Town Residence.	none
Seat.	Strokestown House — County Roscommon Ireland
Date of Birth.	6 Octr 1772
At what period, and to whom succeeded.	Succeeded his Brother Thomas 2d Hartland 10 Decr 1835
Date of Marriage.	married in 1813 Miss Hume of Humewood Co Wicklow She died without issue 11 Decr 1838

DEATH OF LORD HARTLAND.

We have to record the demise of Lord Hartland, who died on Tuesday, the 11th instant, at Strokestown House, county Roscommon. The deceased nobleman was third and youngest son of Maurice, first Lord Hartland, by the Hon. Catherine Moore, daughter of Stephen first Viscount Mount Cashell. His lordship, who was in holy orders, was born 6th of October, 1772, and succeeded to the title on the decease of his brother, Thomas, 8th of December, 1835. He married 24th of November, 1813, Isabella Jane, third daughter of Mr. William Hume, of Humewood, by whom, who died 12th of December, 1838, his lordship had no issue. The title becomes extinct. We understand that Major Mahon, cousin of the deceased lord, will inherit the whole of the landed property.

By the early 1840s Major Denis Mahon (1782–1847) was overseeing the affairs of the estate, although he did not officially inherit until 1845. This form for *Burke's Peerage* (1840) highlights that Major Mahon had indeed assumed control of the estate by this time. Within weeks of the appearance of the potato blight in 1845 the Hartland baronetcy was extinct. In November, on the death of Revd Maurice Mahon, the estate officially passed to Major Denis Mahon.

STROKESTOWN ON THE EVE OF THE FAMINE

Although commonly associated with the Great Famine and there eviction was not an unusual fate for tenants on the Mahon estate in the 1790s

Further adding to the complicated nature of the estate management was the fact that part of the Roscommon properties lay in the hands of the McCausland family of Limavady, county Londonderry, following the marriage of Theodosia Mahon to Connolly McCausland (1754–1822) in 1777. Remarkably, on the eve of the Famine, Marcus McCausland (1787–1862) did not know which properties in Roscommon belonged to him.

Although commonly associated with the Great Famine period, eviction was not an unusual fate for tenants on the Mahon estate from the 1790s onwards. In many cases tenants were evicted and later readmitted as 'caretakers' – eviction being used as a means of frightening them into paying rent.

16 STROKESTOWN AND THE GREAT IRISH FAMINE

STROKESTOWN LOAN FUND.

Account for the Year, ending December 31st, 1839.

Dr.

	£	s.	d.
To Printing Cards, Tickets, Accounts, and Books,	9	1	0
Clerk's Salary,	35	0	0
Porter's do.	6	0	0
A Stamp,		5	0
Fuel and Stationery, for the office,	3	0	0
Lawyer's fees, to defend a Suit against the Clerk, for Cattle seized,		5	0
Car-hire,		8	6
Interest on £600, at 5l. per cent. per ann.	30	0	0
Do. on £200, at 6l. per cent. per ann.	12	0	0
Do. on £250, for 227 days, at 6l. per cent. per ann.	9	6	7
Profits for this year,	44	11	7
	£149	**17**	**8**

Cr.

	£	s.	d.
By Interest on £4735, lent to 2215 borrowers, at 2½ per cent.	118	7	6
By Cash received for Fines,	22	5	7
By Cash received for Application Tickets,	9	4	7
	£149	**17**	**8**

	£	s.	d.
To Cash borrowed from the Treasurer of Loan Funds for the County of Roscommon, as per Note in his hands,	£600	0	0
To Cash borrowed from Major Mahon,	200	0	0
To Profits on the above sums of £800, up to the 31st of Dec., 1838,	97	0	0
To Cash borrowed from Mrs. Mahon,	250	0	0
To Profits from 31st December, 1838, to 31st December, 1839,	44	11	7
	£1191	**11**	**7**

	£	s.	d.
By Cash in the hands of 834 borrowers, and in course of regular weekly payments,	£1175	0	0
By Cash in Treasurer's hands,	16	11	7
	£1191	**11**	**7**

A Classification of Persons Relieved by this Fund from the 31st of Dec. 1838, to the 31st of Dec. 1839:

Land-holders,*	1292
Dealers,	198
Shoe and Brogue-makers,	60
Tailors,	20
Weavers,	61
Smiths,	30
Nailors,	30
Hatters,	33
Masons,	15
Carpenters,	13
Sawyers,	10
Wheel-wrights,	13
Turners,	12
Coopers,	10
Butchers,	26
Labourers,	192
Total,	2215

* NOTE—A great number of these have Horses and Cars, and deal in Corn, Potatoes, Herrings, Salt, &c.

J. BROMELL, PRINTER, BOYLE.

In 1839, in response to the damage caused by the 'Night of the Big Wind', Major Denis Mahon initiated a loan fund. Tenants were expressly forbidden from spending the loan fund money in public houses, an offence for which several were admonished.

Captain Nicholas Mahon, having supported Charles I during the English Civil War, switched allegiance, and later was an officer in a Cromwellian regiment under the command of Charles Coote.[11]

Prior to the Cromwellian Wars of the early 1650s, Mahon had no land holdings in Ireland; by 1670 he possessed thirty-one townlands in county Roscommon.[13] In March

1676 permission was granted to hold fairs at Ballynamully or *Beal na Buille*, and two years later royal consent was given that it would now become known as the manor of Strokestown.[14] By the 1690s the Mahon family had firmly established themselves in Roscommon and began the construction of a house on a grand scale to mirror their new ambitions. The present town, or at least some semblance of what we now see, dates from this time (although part of the town actually lay within the walls of the present demesne). Today, Strokestown remains a striking example of an estate village that formed around, and at the gates of, the 'Big House'.[15]

Little is known of Nicholas Mahon's time in Strokestown. He built a 'chapel of ease', and in its vault he and his Catholic wife, Magdalene French, are buried.[16] Writing in 1930, Olive Pakenham Mahon noted that Nicholas had ordered that his 'children are to be brought up in the fear of God, and the Protestant religion'.[17] He was succeeded in 1680 by his son, John Mahon, a member of parliament for the borough of Jamestown, county Leitrim, in three parliaments 1692, 1695 and 1703. Later, John's son Thomas (1701–82) served in parliament for more than forty years, earning him the title of 'father of the House of Commons'.[18]

The construction of Strokestown Park House began in the 1690s (a date stone, '1696', records the year it was completed), with wings reputedly added by the famed German-born architect Richard Castle, during the lifetime of Thomas Mahon, in the early 1730s.[19] Under the careful guidance of James Donnell, landscape designer, and Martin Connor, head gardener, Strokestown demesne was lavishly enhanced in the mid-1700s with the construction of woodland walks, bridges and a new lawn between the house and the town. The demesne greatly impressed Arthur Young, who wrote in 1779 that the parks in Strokestown were among the finest he had seen in Ireland.[20] A decade later, the gothic arches, a distinctive feature of the demesne, were added.[21] These improvements coincided with the encouragement of an enterprising tenantry of merchants, tradesmen and shopkeepers, who were offered favourable long-term leases in the town in order to promote investment there. In contrast, the conditions of tenants on the wider estate were wretched. According to Young:

> They live on potatoes, milk and butter. Scarce any but what keeps a cow or two. They are not allowed to keep pigs in general, but many will keep a tolerable quantity of poultry. The men dig turf and plant potatoes, and work for their landlord and the women pay the rent by spinning.[22]

Landed estates in Ireland

From the Tudor conquest of the sixteenth century to the early twentieth century, the vast majority of people in Ireland were connected to a landed estate. Estates varied in size from the smallest at 500 acres to large magnates such as Trinity College who, by the mid-nineteenth century, owned close to 190,000 acres. Most landowners rented land to large farmers, who in turn sublet, and by the end of the eighteenth century much of the land of Ireland was in the hands of middlemen who had been granted long and favourable leases. To manage the affairs of an estate, a land agent was employed to carry out the day-to-day business, a system that suited many, including those landlords who resided elsewhere. The landed estate was at the heart of the rural economy in Ireland and the period 1720–1840 arguably represented the golden age of the 'Big House', the residence of landlord families. The 'Big House', as is was termed, was surrounded by an extensive demesne and was an important source of local employment. The residents of these houses lived in opulence when compared to their tenants, but on the eve of the Great Famine many of these great houses were extensively mortgaged. The Famine would exacerbate the owners' financial woes and more than 25 per cent of the land of Ireland changed hands in the early 1850s following the passing of the Encumbered Estates Act in 1849.

Although Ireland was in the middle of an economic boom, Young's description reflected the problems that existed in the country at the end of the eighteenth century; in particular he highlighted the tenants' over-reliance on the potato crop, which would lead to disaster in the mid-1840s.

For the Mahons, though, the pre-Famine years were characterized by continued opulence and spending, as befitting the baronetcy awarded to Maurice Mahon (1738–1819), 1st Baron Hartland, in 1800. In the year of his death Strokestown House was altered significantly by John Lynn, who was also commissioned by Major General Thomas Mahon, 2nd Baron Hartland, to work on other buildings in the town including St John's Church.[23] In his *Statistical survey of the county of Roscommon* (1832), Isaac Weld provides the following description of Strokestown House, or the 'Bawn' as it was referred to locally:

> Originally the house was in the old massive style, so common in the country, with wings advancing at right angles considerably beyond the line of the front; but it underwent an alteration under the direction of Mr Lynn, an English architect, who has contrived to give a light and pleasing appearance to the main or central part of the edifice; but the old wings with their heavy roofs which still remain, detract from the general effect of the whole. The entrance in the central compartment is composed of an Ionic portico, with a flat roof surmounted by a balustrade.[24]

Weld further added that the estate was 'richly wooded ... extensive and in profitable order'.[25]

While Weld may be relied upon for his description of the house and its renovation, his conclusions in regard to the estate's finances could not have been further from the truth. By the time of Thomas Mahon's death in 1835 the estate was financially embarrassed, mainly owing to family settlements, jointures and overspending. For example, a family settlement of 1791 made provision for an annual jointure of £1,000 for the dowager Lady Hartland, the 1st Baron's widow, and £8,000 for their children. Outliving her husband by fifteen years, the dowager Hartland placed considerable financial strain on the estate by her extravagance and longevity; she was ninety-five when she died in 1834.[26] By the mid-1830s the Strokestown estate was almost £30,000

In the pre-Famine decades the practice of subdivision was exacerbated by the population explosion. The townland of Gurtoose on the Mahon estate was a case in point: on the eve of the Famine forty families were farming just over 160 acres, although according to estate records only four families held the lease.

in debt, even though annual estate income had been increasing steadily, from £9,907 in 1827 to £11,473 in 1833.[27] Despite mounting debts, Thomas Mahon continued to promote the building of an Endowed School and the creation of textiles and manufacturing industries. These improvements at Strokestown were evident to a visitor to the town in 1824, who recorded that 'with its white houses [Strokestown] has a very cheerful appearance at a distance; nor is the stranger disappointed when he enters the place as the streets are clean and spacious'.[28] A court house was added in 1832, as was a bridewell (prison), which contained 'apartments for the keeper, a day-room, and cells for the prisoners'.[29] The need for these buildings shows that everything was not idyllic on the estate, and successive owners would struggle to quell local unrest, most particularly that arising from the growth of secret societies and agrarian conspirators.[30]

ROSCOMMON UNION AGRICULTURAL SOCIETY.

REGULATIONS FOR THE

PLOUGHING MATCH,

TO BE HELD AT

MOTE PARK,

ON FRIDAY, THE 23rd OF SEPTEMBER, 1842.

THE FURROW SLICE to be 6 inches deep and 9 inches wide, laid up at an angle of about 45; this gives 24 Furrows, in each 18 foot Set—two of which Sets, 24 Perches long, will make a Rood.

THE SETS to be marked off in the Field with three Poles, one at each end, and one about two Perches from one of the ends.

THE PLOUGHMEN are to assemble at the FARM YARD, MOTE PARK, at 9 o'Clock in the morning, there to draw lots for ground, and immediately afterwards to proceed to the Field.

THE JUDGES are not allowed to go to the Field until the work will be over and all removed therefrom, with the exception of the Ploughs, which are to be left at the end of each division.

No PERSONS, except the Managing Committee, are to be admitted into the Field while the Ploughs are at work; but from the position of the ground, selected as being peculiarly well situated for that purpose, the spectators can view the whole match from a road at the top.

For further particulars relative to the Ploughing Match see the Premium Placards.

BY ORDER,

JOHN CORR, Asst Secty.

Roscommon, 23rd July, 1842.

Thomas French, Printer and Stationer, Society-street, Ballinasloe.

The establishment of agricultural societies in the pre-Famine period was an attempt by land agents and others to introduce new methods of agriculture. Largely resented by the lower orders as 'landlord movements', these societies championed the growing of alternative crops to potatoes including turnip, cauliflower and carrots.

Despite the best efforts of agriculturalists to introduce new crops, more than three million people were entirely dependant on the potato, which could be grown on marginal and inferior soil. The average person was said to have eaten more than 14lbs of potatoes per day!

When the 2nd Baron Hartland died in 1835 without issue, the estate passed to the Revd Maurice Mahon (1772–1845) but his tenure was short lived. Suffering from an attack of paralysis, he was deemed unfit to manage the affairs of the estate and in April 1836, at a *Commission de lunatico inquirendo*, he was declared a lunatic and the estate vested in the Court of Chancery. Describing him as the 'best natural soul that ever graced a pulpit', one contemporary observer speculated that the house of Strokestown would become extinct after his death.[31] It took a nine-year law suit between Marcus McCausland (1787–1862) and Major Denis Mahon to settle who should next inherit the estate. This, of course, added further to the financial woes of the estate.[32] Although he did not officially inherit until November 1845 when the Revd Maurice Mahon died, Major Denis Mahon was resident in Strokestown House as early as 1838 and had begun to implement changes with regard to estate management.[33] To manage the estate, the Court of Chancery appointed receivers, who proved inept and uninterested during this interim period. As a result the Strokestown estate descended into chaos, sparking unrest among tenants who vied for access to land, turbary and other rights.

Despite the presence of receivers and mounting debt, Major Denis Mahon initiated a project of reform and improvement, employing over 500 men in the process.[34] Although court proceedings had not been settled, Mahon was determined that tenants would be brought to order, rents paid and that, in general, the estate would improve. At Tarmonbarry, for example, officials vigilantly watched tenants who were deemed to be withholding rent as a means of protest. Appointing a number of bailiffs and a 'watcher', these men were required to visit tenants on a regular basis, to encourage improvement and to keep an eye on their behaviour.[35] Tenants were warned against burning the land (which was believed to be an effective way of replenishing the soil) and were encouraged to follow those whose 'system of turning small things to good account' would lead to overall improvement. In a number of instances tenants were removed from their holdings when it was deemed that they were not fit to manage the property.[36] Such stringent management of tenants, it was hoped, would also result in the payment of rent and arrears, which by the early 1840s were steadily accumulating.[37]

The 'Night of the Big Wind' (*Oíche na Gaoithe Móire*), which occurred on 6–7 January 1839, was a significant moment in pre-Famine Ireland, yet to date it has received scant attention from historians. The Mahon estate in Roscommon was decimated by the

Lobster Soop

Make a good stock of variety of fresh meats a bit of lean bacon & vegetables particularly celery. Have ready the shells of three good lobsters their coral & the red part that sticks to the shells pound together as fine as you can, strain the stock, then put in the lobster boil it very well for a quar[ter] of an hour strain it thorough a thick sieve or towel add the crust of a french roll cut in small pieces, & let it simmer 'till the bread is soft you may thicken it with a quar[ter] of a pound of fresh butter & a spoonfull of flower browned if I chuse. & some put in the fish of the Lobster cut in pieces.

This receit was got from a gentleman who brought it from germany as the method of making Cray fish soop there. we substituted lobster, & I think it was the best soop I ever saw.

On the eve of the Famine, three successive bad harvests (1840–2) exacerbated the plight of the lower classes, particularly the cottiers and landless labourers. A stark contrast to the reality on the wider estate is reflected in these two documents from Strokestown House. Both dated Christmas 1843, one is a recipe for lobster soup, the other, a list of people to be provided with meat on Christmas day.

List of Persons to get
Pieces of Meat on Christmas Day
1 Tim Neyland ×
2 James O'Hara ×
3 James Mahon ×
4 Cathrine Maguire ×
5 Widow McGovern ×
6 Nanny Quinn ×
7 Polly McNiel
8 Mrs Jamieson ×
9 Widow Carley
10 Peggy Hagan
~~11 Ingram (Gate Porter)~~
12 old Cowen × (Church Street)
13 Billy Geraghty ×
~~14 Paddy Kenny~~ Dead
15 Barkey Farrell ×
11 McKenzie. Gate Porter
1. ic Conboy. Longford Gate
.. Kenny. Plough Man

Total 16

As Many of those as are living
are to have a Piece of Meat
22d Decr 42   D. Mahon

Major Denis Mahon, described by Cecil Woodham Smith in *The Great Hunger* as 'amiable and likeable'.

most severe storm of the nineteenth century, which swept in from the west coast in the afternoon of 6 January. At Strokestown House trees and plants were uprooted, while the walled garden and outbuildings were severely damaged. But the most significant damage was inflicted on the thousands of landless labourers and cottiers, many of whom were living on the edges of the bog or huddled in makeshift accommodation across the estate. The 'Big Wind' also marked a turning point in Major Denis Mahon's involvement in the estate and laid the foundations for much of the unrest witnessed in the 1840s. While much of the destruction has gone unrecorded, the large number of applicants for relief from the Strokestown Loan Fund operated by Major Denis Mahon gives an indication of the effect that the storm had locally.[38] As a result of the destitution caused by the storm a loan scheme was initiated, the terms of which were strict and were said to keep tenants perpetually bound to the landlord.[39] For example, tenants were forbidden to spend money in public houses (for which several were admonished) and no money was loaned until previous loans had been repaid in full.[40] Ironically, in the majority of cases, Major Denis Mahon was the ultimate recipient as many tenants used these funds to pay their rent. Not surprisingly contemporary commentators condemned the practice of loan funds.[41]

Three disastrous wet summers followed, during which time the harvest was rarely saved. With the frequent failure of the potato crop (it has been estimated that from 1700 to 1845 there were twenty-seven partial failures), it was hardly surprising that a large arrear had accumulated on the Strokestown rental. By 1844, many tenants were four years in arrears. Overcrowding, subdivision and the scarcity of conacre all resulted in intense pressure on land. As a result many chose emigration as a means of escaping the endemic poverty.[42]

Seasonal working migration was key to the survival of many families. Crucially, employment networks in England, Scotland and Wales existed before the Famine that seasonal workers were able to utilize.[43] In 1835 it was estimated that at least 150 people from Strokestown sought seasonal work in England. Family members remaining behind were left to fend for themselves, to 'drag out a miserable existence' from their own exertions.

A large majority of tenants, as noted by Terence Shanley, medical attendant for the Tarmonbarry and Kilglass dispensary, endured habitual disease and many simply lingered from day to day in fear of dying. In three years he estimated that he had attended to over 10,000 people where 'fevers of almost every type, affections of the chest, rheumatism, small-pox, measles, whooping cough, croup, dysentery, diarrhoea, cholera' prevailed.[44] Moreover, a government report highlighted the 'entire neglect' of the Strokestown area during the cholera outbreak of 1832. As many as sixty people died in the town's dispensary and there was no one who would remove the dead. In most cases the poor and dying huddled together, unable to move. Those of means, it was claimed, had fled on the first report of the disease and for several weeks the town was deserted; there were no fairs or markets and no business transacted. Such apathy apparently stemmed from the fact that 'the town was owned by a nobleman absentee for ten months of the year and no information could be gathered from the agent'.[45]

For those who remained poverty was ever present. As early as 1809 such was the poverty at Strokestown that the British politician, Edward Wakefield, denounced the local agent for the condition of the people:

> I found everywhere, cabins of the most wretched aspect, infamous stone roads, very minute divisions of lands and, what usually follows it, a superabundant but miserable people. I do not recollect to have traveled so many miles through any estate in Ireland which presented such a scene of desolation, and nothing astonished me so much as the multitude of poverty-struck inhabitants, from whom I could learn very little other than that the estate belonged to 'My Lord', whom they loathed with imprecations.[46]

So overcrowded were holdings that several generations lived side by side, all trying to eke out a living from the land, the townland of Gortoose being a case in point. On the eve of the Famine forty families were farming just over 160 acres at Gortoose, although according to estate records only four families held leases.[47] The prevalence of middlemen who sublet the land to a host of under-tenants was also problematic; in many cases no leases were issued and thus the vast majority of people had no recourse to the law and could be ejected at a moment's notice. In 1831, for example, the expiration of a middleman's lease resulted in the eviction of twenty-eight families, prompting Thomas Conry, then agent, to state:

> In all my life I never performed so disagreeable a duty, the poor creatures quit it with extreme reluctance, still they were perfectly obedient to the law. It will remain tenantless for the year as no person would venture to take it.[48]

Conry's assertion that the land would remain tenantless was correct as it was the unwritten rule of nineteenth-century Ireland that land from which tenants had been evicted was to be avoided. To do otherwise risked invoking the wrath of secret societies, whose orders were strictly obeyed. Indeed, much of the pre-Famine crime and outrage stemmed from these societies' activities.

Religious animosity in the pre-Famine decades also helped create deep division within Roscommon society. Sometimes the community split along religious lines, and this was detrimental to those most in need when the Famine struck. As early as

August 1817 a memorial sent to the lord lieutenant warned that all the Protestants in Strokestown were to be murdered, while there were also regular boycotts of Protestant shops:

> We bid no person or persons whatsoever to buy any commodity from any of the villainous crew calling themselves Orangemen. Now depend on it that there will be a proper watch set for to mark all those that will dare to attempt to go inside the doors of the persons herein mentioned first that upstart orange scoundrel Boyd.[49]

Despite these threats, Strokestown was annually bedecked with Orange lilies in advance of 12 July celebrations, which irked a largely Catholic population. The Revd Michael McDermott, parish priest of Strokestown (1825–66), lambasted what he believed to be the religious bigotry of the gentry and defended his parishioners at all opportunities.[50]

With rising poverty it was perhaps to be expected that crime and outrage spiralled out of control. Strokestown, and by extension county Roscommon, was among the worst affected areas in Ireland (only counties Tipperary, Clare, Limerick and Leitrim were considered more violent).[51] Indeed, simmering discontent was evident in Strokestown in the early 1840s as small farmers and landless labourers clamoured for access to land. This situation was exacerbated by the fact that Roscommon had one of the highest population densities in the country – the period 1732 to 1821 witnessed a 300% increase.[52] Making the most of the newly implemented Irish Poor Law Act of 1838, and the provisions it brought for the establishment of workhouses, landlords in Roscommon began to clear the land of paupers and those who were deemed unlikely to ever improve their situation. The number of evictions increased following the heated general elections of 1841 and were widely castigated:

> The work of depopulation is progressing with railroad celerity. At the quarter sessions in Strokestown not less than 104 ejectments were entered for the purpose of ridding the properties of noblemen and gentlemen of the pauper population.[53]

> **THE CON-ACRE DISTURBANCES.**
> (FROM A PRIVATE CORRESPONDENT.)
> Strokestown, April 1st, 1845.
>
> On yesterday we had another adjournment of the inquest on the body of poor Gavagin, who was shot by the police near this town. The coroner directed the jury to be in attendance on Monday, the 7th of this month, to resume their inquiry. The people are very much dissatisfied at those adjournments, believing that there is not sufficient grounds for the coroner's so doing, and the very great excitement that prevails is not likely to subside by procrastinating the investigation. At the commencement of the proceedings on yesterday the coroner demanded a list of those witnesses the friends of the deceased intended to examine. This he did at the request of counsel for the police. The counsel for the deceased objected to this mode of proceeding, and said he would not be concluded by any list of witnesses handed in—that it was contrary to custom and law—that at a coroner's inquest the names in such a list (if any were

With access to land an integral concern for a huge proportion of the population, the conacre was very important. Here, land was leased on the eleven-months system, which meant that there was no legal entitlement for tenants to be given access from year to year. This, in turn, led to growing unrest, and as in the case of 'poor Gavigan' here, to crime and disorder.

Eviction prompted an immediate response, and if ejected tenants elsewhere were slow to take matters into their own hands, the same cannot be said of the people of Roscommon. The attempted assassination of Richard Irwin, a justice of the peace, in October 1843, was an example of this and was followed by the shooting of his brother and agent, Valentine, who had been on his way to 'drive' for rent on lands at Fairymount, near Strokestown. A man named Brooks was murdered there over the taking of land in 1842.[54] Intimidation and violence took on other forms, with house burnings the favoured tactic of agrarian conspirators.[55] In June 1844, Patrick Hughes, a pensioner, was murdered at Strokestown by four men who stabbed him and cracked his skull; the motives for this murder were said to be land related.[56] The murder prompted one commentator to add that 'the state of society is such in the county of Roscommon that no man can reckon his life for one moment with safety', while another believed that although the people appeared friendly, they were in fact 'deep and distant'.[57]

This litany of crime continued. Patrick Sheil, a farmer, was murdered in January 1845 when he tried to raise the price of oats he was selling at the local market.[58] Two months later the *Freeman's Journal* reported the continuing conflict between the police and the 'peasantry' in Strokestown.[59] Houses were raided for weapons, while in June the Revd McDermott was called on by the police to break up a riot that had developed in the town. By early September mobs had resorted to the mutilation of cattle, sheep and other animals, while violent and vicious attacks on homes and people continued.

There was also widespread anger over the shooting by the police of a man named Gavigan during disturbances over access to conacre.[60] This shooting at Ballinafad occurred when over 300 men gathered to dig up a field of potatoes as a means of intimidation, and were attacked by police in the process. Later, banditti attacked the houses of John and Michael Dignan, and shot dead Michael, who was a poor rate collector.[61] Although over 100 men were working in nearby fields none came forward to offer any information.[62]

These were not the only problems that created local tension on the eve of the Famine. There was also widespread resentment towards the clergy over prices for conducting weddings, funerals and christenings.[63] Already hard pressed, the inhabitants of Strokestown were also expected to contribute to various religious and political collections. In 1845, for example, amid impending famine, Catholic parishioners contributed to the Association for the Propagation of the Faith, while local repeal wardens regularly collected 'O'Connell's Rent'.[64]

As September 1845 dawned, despite the best efforts of Major Denis Mahon, his agent and bailiffs, the estate rental continued to show mounting arrears. In some cases tenants had not paid any rent since 1840 and the difficulties in management were exemplified by the return of many of those who had been evicted in 1841.[65] In addition, attempts to prevent the burning and subdivision of land had largely failed. As the summer of 1845 came to a close crime and poverty prevailed. Despairing of the plight of the people around Slieve Bawn and Strokestown in general, a correspondent to the *Freeman's Journal* lamented that 'our population here has increased awfully. Their poverty and their patience are commensurate. All they seem to ask is roots and salt for their subsistence'.[66] Conditions for those on the Strokestown estate were about to get much worse.

From 1700 until 1845 the potato crop failed more than 27 times. As a result, according to the novelist William Carleton, 'no year was without famine'. Accordingly, in 1845 many believed there was no cause for alarm, and that they simply had to wait for the next crop.

The landed estate was at the heart of the rural economy in Ireland and the period 1720-1840 is represented the golden age of 'Big House', the residence of landlord families. The 'Big House', as is was termed, was surrounded by an extensive demesne and wa

2

'The Poorest Peasantry on the Face of the Earth': Early Relief Efforts, 1846-7

> The people in this district are in the most awful state of destitution, many of them having pawned every article belonging to them — some have died from starvation — provisions are at famine price — hunger has forced them to slaughter and carry away sheep, and unless those who have been blessed by Providence with the means, come forward promptly and liberally, the most dreadful consequence are sure to ensue.[1]

In November 1845 the Revd Maurice Mahon, 3rd Baron Hartland, died, thereby handing official control of the estate to Major Denis Mahon.[2] With the estate almost £30,000 in debt, it was a poisoned chalice to inherit. Perusing the estate rentals made for bleak reading and in many cases tenants had not paid their rent in almost five years. Now, with the impending disaster of a failed potato crop, there was little hope of receiving rents, while resources needed to alleviate poverty were particularly stretched. For many in Strokestown, the memories of previous 'famines' and periods of disease and distress were all too recent. They also recalled the failure of the resident gentry and people of means to provide relief. In 1822, for example, during a period of acute distress following the partial failure of the potato crop, a resolution passed by the 'principled

STR/1096.

Strokestown Sept 12th 1846

The following Persons are this day Recommended to constitute the New Relief Committee for the Parishes of Bumlin, Kiltrustan and Lissanuffy, in the Barony of Roscommon & County of Roscommon pursuant to the Provisions of the Amended Act of 10 Vic. Cap 107 –

1. D M Stratton DL LP Co Ror
2. Thos Conry
3. Thos Dillon
4. Dan'l Hughes
5. John Hague
6. Mich'l O'Bierne
7. Bart'w Mahon

RELIEF FUND.

LEABEG, BALLYMOE,
County Roscommon,
3d November, 1846.

Sir,

As Secretary to the RELIEF COMMITTEE for the Parishes of BALLINTOBBER, DRIMATEMPLE, and that part of BALLINAKILL in the County Roscommon, I have been requested to apply to you, as Proprietor of the Lands of _____ in the Parish of _____ for a SUBSCRIPTION to the RELIEF FUND for those Parishes.

The people in this District are in the most awful state of destitution, many of them having pawned every article belonging to them—some have died from starvation—provisions are at famine price—hunger has forced them to slaughter and carry away sheep, and unless those who have been blessed by Providence with the means, come forward promptly and liberally, the most dreadful consequence are sure to ensue.

An early reply will oblige your obedient servant,

J. IRWIN,
Secretary Relief Committee for Parishes
of Ballintobber, &c.

(*Left*) Reformed in September 1846, the Strokestown relief committee reflected the public feeling that this was now a deepening crisis and that the exertions of a large body of public representatives was needed to alleviate hunger and destitution.

(*Above*) By the end of 1846 many people complained that a 'famine fatigue' had set in with regard the provision of relief. This circular by John Irwin highlights that many were using the Famine to their own advantage and that food was hoarded so as to make the best possible profits, thereby preventing those most in need from accessing supplies.

although forty men working on the scheme were witness to the crime, none would provide evidence.[22] It mattered little that those employed on the public works were left without pay as a result. Others were forced from work through intimidation; 600 members of a secret society, the Molly Maguires, assembled at the Roscommon–Leitrim border, preventing men from carrying out work on a bridge across the river Shannon.[23]

Alarm in Roscommon had now turned to panic. Newspapers continued to report the absolute dearth of food in the county: 'in a fortnight not one of the tenantry will have a potato' and only the early exertions of the former British Prime Minister, Sir Robert Peel, in secretly importing Indian corn, it was claimed, had averted a 'fierce famine'.[24] These feelings were all too clear to the Revd Michael McDermott who 'could not fully describe the alarm that was felt in the Strokestown area from the high price of potatoes and from where the people express their discontent in a menacing manner and nothing is heard except threats and murmurs'.[25]

The almost-daily distribution of relief (Indian corn) during the summer months did stem the tide of death, but even this provision of relief was fraught with difficulties and problems. Surviving documentation in the Strokestown Park archive sheds light on the people who were relieved daily during these months but also raises awkward questions about those who took relief and were not entitled to do so. Indeed, impersonation and false claims for relief would come to characterize the Famine at a local level. As a means of establishing order in the provision of relief, investigations concluded that a number of people on the Mahon estate were unworthy of receiving relief. These included, for example, James Grace who was found to be getting money from America and so was struck off the list, as was Celia Rush of Scramogue whose father owned land. Others used aliases to acquire rations. One man claiming to be 'John Kearns of Scramogue' was found to be lying as no such person existed, while the McKeon girls of North Yard, four in all, were struck off when it was discovered that their father was in England and they had plenty of money. It was a problem that could not be fully overcome though, and in 1848 was still troubling the Strokestown estate. As a means of ascertaining who was genuine, James Gray, an engineer on the board of works, sought a quarry to 'test the able-bodied workers on the public works' as to how much they really needed relief.[26]

The provision of relief to those most in need was at times protracted and complicated. Landlords and their agents continually argued over boundaries and under whose care certain paupers fell. There was also considerable acrimony over the appointment of officials on the public work schemes. As Major Denis Mahon's newly appointed estate agent, John Ross Mahon (no relation), highlighted, this squabbling

Although Major Denis Mahon had inherited an estate in 1845 that was in serious financial difficulty, he endeavoured to provide relief for his starving tenantry. Throughout 1846, and with limited resources, he laboured to relieve the plight of more than 4,000 people on a weekly basis. Some were provided with relief gratuitously, and some at half price, as shown in the list above for the townlands of Leitrim, Dooherty and Curnahsina.

EARLY RELIEF EFFORTS, 1846–7

To overcome the problem of mismanagement, in 1846 John Ross Mahon, of the Dublin land agency firm Guinness & Mahon, was appointed as land agent. Within two years of his arrival Ross Mahon had drastically altered the landscape of Roscommon.

didn't help the tenants who 'were all absolutely starving'.[27] Indeed, it was even claimed that 'several families contriving to make food of bran go into the fields to pluck the wild herbs for their subsistence'.[28] Recalling these months, William Parks, a tenant, would later write that many of the paupers died and the houses became dilapidated.[29]

With relief supplies at Strokestown decreasing, the signs were ominous. The great fair of Ballinafad, south of Strokestown, at the end of August 1846 was badly attended, the quality of stock was poor and the animals on the village green were said to be of an 'inferior class'.[30] Roscommon was now 'far worse off than neighbouring Mayo', a county notoriously affected by poverty.[31]

There was also evidence of a change in attitudes among the landlords and gentry of the county. Some, like Major Denis Mahon, were reluctant to blame the distress on the failure of the potato alone, believing that it was also caused from 'the very large and overgrown population of this district'.[32] Stretched to the limits, Major Mahon and others sought the help of the central relief committee in Dublin as to how best to proceed.[33] While holding out the 'sanguine hope' of further contributions locally – in July 1846 over eighty-five people had given subscriptions – Mahon also looked to

What was the potato blight? Causes of the Famine

By the mid-nineteenth century more than three million people in Ireland were entirely dependent on the potato as their staple food. The potato, which could be grown with great success on poor and inferior soil, was prone to failure and over the previous 150 years there had been numerous lost harvests. In 1843 the first signs of *Phytophthora infestans*, or the potato blight as it is more commonly known, were noticed in South America. It spread to Europe the following year. The potato blight is a fungal infection which thrives in damp, mild weather conditions. It had not been previously experienced in Europe, but by late 1845 it affected the crop in much of central Europe, Scandinavia, Scotland and parts of south-west England. Its appearance in Ireland in September 1845 was to have disastrous consequences. On 13 September the *Gardener's Chronicle* reported: 'we stop the press with very great regret to announce that the potato murrain has unequivocally declared itself in Ireland'.

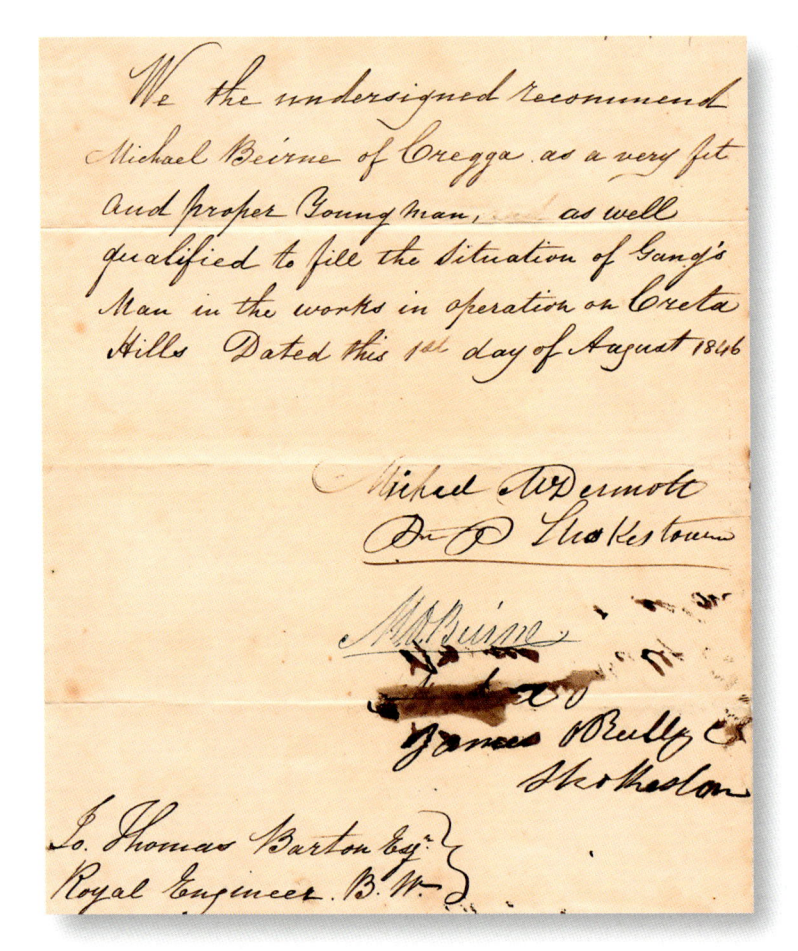

> We the undersigned recommend Michael Beirne of Cregga as a very fit and proper Young man, and as well qualified to fill the situation of Gang's Man in the works in operation on Creta Hills Dated this 1st day of August 1846
>
> Michael McDermott
> Dr P Strokestown
>
> M Beirne
>
> James Reilly
> Strokestown
>
> To Thomas Barton Esq.
> Royal Engineer. B.W.

As a means of relieving local poverty, men, women and children were put together on the public work schemes, often breaking stones, laying roadways and carrying out other heavy manual work. Employment on the scheme, in particular situations like 'ganger' and 'foreman', was highly sought after.

other ways of providing relief, and also of restoring some semblance of stability to his estate. He confided in his former agent, Thomas Conry, that he had 'attacked the Catholic bishop and clergy assembled here [in Strokestown] – they have been feasting & stuffing and praying here the last week'.[34] While it is difficult to verify Major Mahon's account (he was in London at this time), there may have been some truth in the suggestion that the relief committee and those of means were not attending to their duties as they should. It is remarkable to think that in the midst of such poverty and want that the famed races of Lenabane, near Roscommon town, took place before a huge attendance in August 1846.[35] Similarly, the collection of the Repeal rent for Daniel O'Connell remained steadfast during this period, while the building of Kiltrustan church drew heavily on local finances.[36]

By the end of the summer of 1846, and with the second failure of the potato crop dawning, the situation was nearing breaking point. In August, tenants in the

By the beginning of 1847 many of Major Denis Mahon's tenants ha[d fled] to the workhouse in Roscommon town.

A number of tenants who owed rent for more than five years were targeted in the early wave of evictions on the Mahon estate. These people, according to Major Denis Mahon, were never likely to recover and were using the potato blight as an excuse for their own failure. Here, as this document shows, tenants in arrears at Kildalogue are being selected for ejection.

By the beginning of 1847 many of Major Denis Mahon's tenants had fled to the workhouse in Roscommon town. The failure of the resident gentry to contribute to relief efforts was criticized by Mahon and others but they could do little in persuading those of means to help.

EARLY RELIEF EFFORTS, 1846–7   43

Petitions form a large corpus of the Strokestown archive and offer a remarkable insight into the lives of many of those tenants who were severely affected by the Famine. Those of the Widow Cox and Pat Wallace highlight the many vicissitudes that people endured during the Famine period.

In Roscommon, as elsewhere, the failure to collect poor law rates, as illustrated in the case of Marcus McCausland above, ultimately led to the withdrawing of relief for those most in need. By the end of 1847, with many poor law unions bankrupt, relief measures had collapsed.

CAPTAIN ROCK'S BANDITTI SWEARING IN A NEW MEMBER

With a rent strike in place on the Crown estate at Ballykilcline (see p. 51), secret societies at Strokestown (in particular, the feared Molly Maguires) orchestrated resistance to the collection of rent on the Mahon estate.

townland of Cloonahee petitioned Thomas Conry and neighbouring landowners, including Sir John Conry, for help. Reminding Conry of the failure of the gentry and those of means to provide relief, the petition further stated:

> Gentlemen you know little of the state of the suffering poor … are we to resort to outrage. Gentlemen we fear that the peace of the country will be much disturbed if relief be not immediately, more extensively afforded to the suffering peasantry. We are not joining in anything illegal or contrary to the laws of the God or the land unless pressed to by HUNGER.

This petition also highlighted that the social background of those affected by famine was slowly changing. A similar petition from the 'Tradesmen of Strokestown', submitted in September, sought employment and relief, and contained the names of eighty-four men who were hitherto unaffected by the calamity. The ensuing winter was one of the worst on record. Snow and ice remained on the ground for nearly three months, leaving many areas impassable and making it impossible to deliver relief to those in need. An English visitor, in the company of the Society of Friends, noted the utter starvation of the people of Roscommon and in an interview with Lord Lorton at Boyle, the latter expressed fears that if the relief works were stopped the people of the county would rise up and plunder all of the property. 'Famine was written on the faces of these women' he concluded.[37] In the same month the people of Strokestown were described as being 'half starved already' and it was wondered 'what will become of them'.[38]

Worryingly for those most in need, new conditions were laid down by the Strokestown relief committee: relief was only to be given to those 'industriously inclined and not connected with the non-payment of rent'. The withholding of rent had spread from the nearby Crown estate at Ballykilcline.[39] Naturally, decisions like these had disastrous consequences for those unconnected with the rent strike and who were now in a state of starvation. As 1847 began, those who succumbed to starvation included Michael Cox of Kilgaffin, whose inquest concluded that he had died from 'hunger and destitution', and John Lyons of North Yard in Strokestown, whose decayed remains were 'found in the walls of Brackens house'.[40] These two deaths would be followed by hundreds more.

During the summer of 1846, over 4,000 people were relieved weekly thanks mainly to the efforts of local subscribers. Detailed lists that survive in the Strokestown archive highlight the distances people travelled to be given relief.

3

'Destitution Prevails on this Country': Changing Attitudes on the Mahon Estate

> I have the honour to inform you that in consequence of the very great distress which exists in this town and the want of food for the poor as well as want of employment. The inhabitants have again raised a subscription amongst themselves for the charitable purpose of giving them relief by work but our funds are too small.[1]

> It strikes me that it is not fair for those who have had their profits for years to turn short on the landlord when they find the times get bad.[2]

As hunger and distress grew, so too did crime and social disorder. The resident gentry bemoaned the fact that 'life and property' were not protected and questioned what use the police were and 'what more necessary duty can they perform'.[3] As 1847 began almost all of the board of works projects in Roscommon were reported to have stopped, their resources exhausted. Querying the exertions of local committees, the *Roscommon Journal* wondered 'what in the name of god is our local committee doing? Will they prefer having the country disturbed, their cattle slaughtered, their

In August 1846 Major Denis Mahon appealed to the Relief Commissioners at Dublin Castle for assistance on account of the 'very great distress which exists in this town'. It was obvious to all concerned that local subscriptions alone could not alleviate the poverty that prevailed.

lives endangered by a starving peasantry, driven to madness by destitution?'[4] The sense of hopelessness as expressed by the newspaper editor was evident elsewhere as anarchy prevailed. In his Lenten pastorals the Roman Catholic bishop of Elphin, George Browne (1795–1858), castigated the banditti, or what he called the 'deluded' characters, who were associated with the 'accursed and illegal system of Molly Maguire' and other secret societies.[5] For the majority of people, the Molly Maguires and their counterparts were a feared and unwanted group who frequently took the

> **MEETING OF TRADESMEN IN STROKESTOWN—PUBLIC DISTRESS.**
> (FROM A CORRESPONDENT).
> A meeting of poor tradesmen was held in the Reading-room of this town on Tuesday evening,
> Mr. JAMES GRADY in the chair,
> when, after some statements as to the present condition and future prospects of the poor of that locality, the following resolutions were agreed to:—
> "Resolved—That a deputation be formed of this meeting to submit to the magistrates, cesspayers, and gentlemen composing the adjourned baronial meeting to be held this day in the Court-house of Strokestown the state of our inability to maintain our families, through the failure of our business, which arises from universal distress.
> "Resolved—That we deem it expedient that we should get up a petition to his Excellency the Lord Lieutenant, expressive of our present state of destitution, occasioned by distress, unfortunately too general in this town and surrounding country, through the failure of the potato.
> "Resolved—That the following address be presented to his Excellency the Lord Lieutenant, subject to the opinion

Signed by eighty-four people, the petition of the tradesmen of Strokestown in September 1846 highlighted the effect that the second failure of the potato had on all classes. (*FJ*, 25 Sept. 1846).

law into their own hands and meted out their own form of punishment.[6] However, it was not just the Molly Maguires who had resorted to crime, and the number of criminal cases brought before the Strokestown petty sessions reflected this. As a result of the rise in criminal proceedings Strokestown magistrates suspended the use of the jaunting car that conveyed prisoners to Roscommon gaol as it had become too expensive, instead making prisoners walk after they had been sentenced![7]

This upsurge in social disorder coincided with the first clearance of tenants near Strokestown in October 1846. Patrick Browne, a brother of the aforementioned Bishop George Browne, evicted several families who were in arrears of rent. Browne, a justice of the peace and later a member of the Strokestown Board of Guardians, was reputedly the only person in Roscommon who looked for the May 'gale' of 1846.[8] However, the number of civil bills and ejectment proceedings brought before the courts by the end of 1846 indicated that landlords and agents were starting to take a more hard-lined approach.[9] With trouble brewing in the neighbouring parish of Kilglass, a rent strike eventually spilled over onto the Mahon estate.

From the 1790s until 1834 the Mahon family had leased the townland of Ballykilcline, in the parish of Kilglass, but, unable to renegotiate terms with the Crown, the estate reverted to the control of the Commissioners of Woods, Forests, Land Revenues, Works and Buildings.[10] The townland of Ballykilcline consisted of 602 acres on the edge of Kilglass lake and on the eve of the Famine more than 500 people combined

Acting as treasurer for the Strokestown relief committee, Major Denis Mahon appealed to the gentry and those of means to contribute. His former agent, Thomas Conry, was scolded in 1846 for failing to do so. Much of the early relief was provided by the Mahon family as the list of subscribers in July 1846 confirms (*left*). With local resources exhausted, the Strokestown relief committee appealed elsewhere. This list of subscribers for early March 1847 (*below*) shows that money was forthcoming from the British Relief Association, the Society of Friends, Birmingham relief committee and Dr Biggs in London.

52 STROKESTOWN AND THE GREAT IRISH FAMINE

to thwart the collection of rent there.[11] For many years tenants had been left to their own devices and the estate was said to have been the 'most mismanaged in Ireland' with poverty endemic.[12] By the mid-1830s Ballykilcline had become notorious for its lawlessness and neglected appearance. The antiquarian, John O'Donovan, wrote that the parish of Kilglass was 'proverbial in this part of the country for its wickedness'. Perhaps more tellingly, George Knox, the Crown's agent, believed them to be the 'most lawless and violent set of people in the county of Roscommon'.[13] Here justice was meted out by the local secret society who were not afraid to punish those who were deemed to break the local 'code'. Just as at nearby Strokestown, the Molly Maguires operated in a vicious and unrelenting manner, as the punishment meted out to Patrick Reilly in 1842 indicated (Reilly's house was attacked and burnt).[14] These 'armed mollys in female attire' roamed the countryside, striking fear and terror into the community.[15] For the Mahon estate this had serious implications, not least because of the burden placed on the local committee who were charged with the provision of relief, but also because the resistance to the payment of rent was soon to be replicated all across Strokestown.

The situation at Ballykilcline had become worse by 1844 when the doors of the twelve leaders of the rent strike, known as 'the defendants', were bolted to try to keep them out of their cottages. This was never likely to succeed, and as George Knox concluded 'nothing short of levelling the houses of these refractory people will ever bring them into subjection'.[16] In May 1847 ejectment notices were eventually issued against the Ballykilcline tenants and accompanied by the bailiffs and agent, a party of twenty dragoons sent from Dublin Castle oversaw the proceedings.[17] By this time most tenants owed between nine and twelve years rent.[18] The Ballykilcline tenants were evicted in four groups, beginning in September 1847, and ending in March 1848.[19] Travelling to Dublin, and then to Liverpool, the emigrants, 366 in all, embarked for New York. In time, the evictions at Ballykilcline and the clearances on the Mahon estate blurred together in local memory. For some, the murder of Major Denis Mahon in November 1847 was legitimized by the harsh treatment of those involved in the Ballykilcline 'rebellion'. Indeed, there is every likelihood that the plan to murder Mahon originated, or at the very least was encouraged, in Ballykilcline.[20] Undoubtedly, the rent strike at Ballykilcline emboldened Major Denis Mahon's tenants to do likewise; this course of action was to end in disastrous consequences for both parties.

Major Denis Mahon was keen to avoid the public censure that had followed from the large-scale clearance of tenants on other estates in 1846, particularly on the Gerrard estate in county Galway. Here Marcella Gerrard was publicly condemned for her treatment of tenants, so much so that the term 'Gerrardising' came to be associated with other Famine evictions.[21] While some landlords implemented 'estate rules' as a means of avoiding public condemnation, Mahon targeted the removal of tenants by middlemen.[22] However, it was the clearances that Mahon himself oversaw that were to have a lasting impact. Realizing he was losing control of his estate and that there was little hope of ever receiving the mounting arrears, Mahon opted to appoint the professional land agency firm Guinness & Mahon, relieving his land agent Thomas Conry of his duties.[23] The firm, headed by Ross Mahon and Robert Rundell Guinness, was based in South Frederick Street, Dublin, and along with Messrs Stewart and Kincaid, was among the most prolific in the agency business in the mid-nineteenth century. In October 1846 the arrival of John Ross Mahon as agent heralded a new departure in terms of management style and also influenced how the Mahon family would come to be portrayed in later times.[24] Providing a bond of £5,000 as security for the agency, Ross Mahon later recalled his arrival at the estate:

> When I became agent to the Strokestown estate in 1846, it was covered with paupers. The rental was £9,000 a year, exclusive of the demesne. The average quantity of land each tenant held was three acres one rood plantation measure, without counting under-tenants, and almost every tenant had one or two under-tenants.[25]

Having surveyed the estate and thoroughly investigated the estate accounts (which confirmed that in most cases tenants had paid no rent in four or five years), his conclusion was straightforward: it would be better to let the land lie waste for a year than let paupers remain.[26] In a detailed memorandum to his employer, he candidly outlined his findings:

> Emigration on an extensive scale was the principal feature of my plan – as while the large and completely pauperised population which was on the estate remained, rent could not be collected, nor could any system for the amelioration of the condition of the people be introduced.[27]

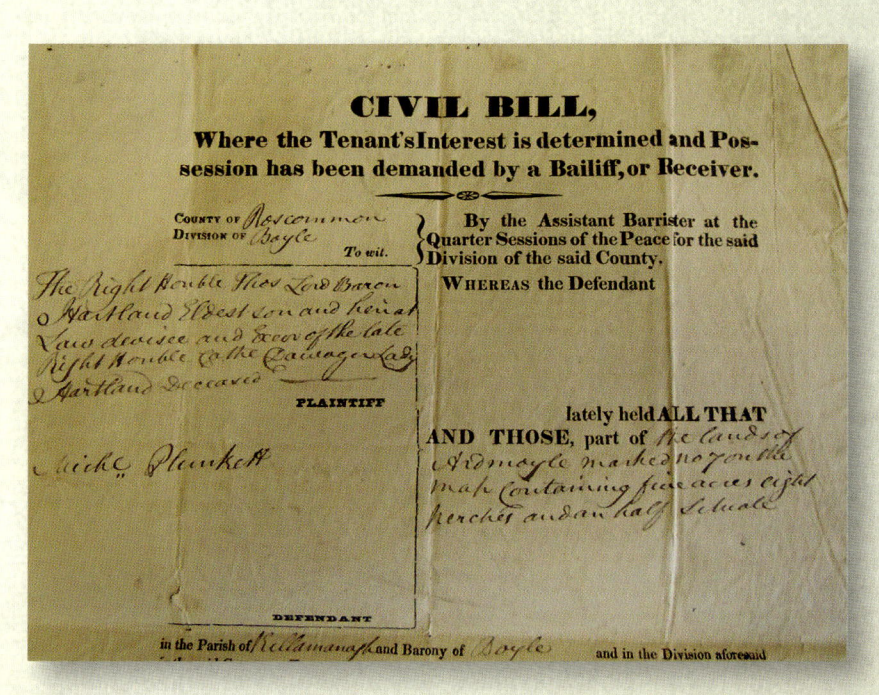

As the Famine wore on the delivery and posting of these bills became extremely dangerous and in some instances bailiffs could not be found to do these jo...

CIVIL BILL,
Where the Tenant's Interest is determined and Possession has been demanded by a Bailiff, or Receiver.

County of *Roscommon*
Division of *Boyle*
To wit.

By the Assistant Barrister at the Quarter Sessions of the Peace for the said Division of the said County.

WHEREAS the Defendant

PLAINTIFF: The Right Honble Thos Lord Baron O Hartland Eldest son and heir at Law devisee and Exor of the late Right Honble the Dowager Lady O Hartland Deceased

DEFENDANT: Mick. Plunkett

lately held ALL THAT AND THOSE, part of *the lands of Ardmoyle marked no 7 on the map containing five acres eight perches and an half Irish*

in the Parish of *Killamanagh* and Barony of *Boyle* and in the Division aforesaid

NOTICE TO QUIT.

TAKE NOTICE, that I do hereby require you to deliver up to Me, or to my Attorney, ~~Agent~~, or Bailiff lawfully authorised thereto, on the *First* day of *May* next ensuing the date hereof, the Quiet and Peaceable Possession of ALL THAT AND THOSE *the House and lands of Curradrehid which you hold of Lieutenant Gilbert Mahon of Her Majesty's Ninety Fourth Regiment of Foot now Quartered in the East Indies* situate in the Parish of *Lissonuffy* Barony of *Roscommon* and County of *Roscommon* now in your Possession as Tenant from Year to Year, provided your Tenancy originally commenced at that time of the year, and if otherwise, that you surrender and deliver up to me the possession of the said Premises at the end of the year of your Tenancy, which shall expire next after the end of half-a-year from the time of your being served with this Notice, and in case you shall refuse or neglect to deliver up said Premises, I will proceed to recover possession, and double the yearly value thereof, and all Costs attending such recovery.

Dated this *31st* day of *October*
One Thousand Eight Hundred and Forty- *Nine*

To
Widow Mary Campbell
of Curradrehid

Barthw Mahon
Agent to *Gilbert Mahon*
the Landlord of said Premises

A Civil Bill for ejectment or 'Notice to Quit' was issued to the tenant usually about six months before the eviction. As the Famine wore on, the delivery and posting of these bills became extremely dangerous, and in some instances bailiffs could not be found to do these jobs.

CHANGING ATTITUDES ON THE MAHON ESTATE

Secret societies

In the 1760s, a series of land-related disturbances, centred mainly on Tipperary and known as 'Whiteboyism', occurred throughout the country. By the 1790s, groups such as the Defenders terrorized the countryside, opposing the payment of taxes, tithes and rents. These were local oath-bound societies in which secrecy was paramount and members were often disguised when carrying out attacks. Economic decline in the post-Napoleonic era increased the pressure for land, giving rise to the growth of secret societies (including groups such as the Caravats, Shanavests and Rockites) whose agendas were driven by the need to control the agrarian economy. Cottiers and the landless often used the cloak of secret societies to demand employment, better wages and access to conacre. In many instances, familial and local disputes were settled with the involvement of the local secret society. By the early 1840s the violent nature of groups such as the Carders and Molly Maguires meant that secret societies were both feared and detested.

As the tenants had done at Ballykilcline, combinations formed at Strokestown against the payment of rent. Even where tenants had the means to pay rent, they were encouraged by threat and intimidation to withhold payment. According to Major Mahon, the people joined with 'alacrity in the combination' and it was 'carried on with so much determination'. Ross Mahon was determined to break the rent strike and in his first few months at Strokestown devoted his energies to doing so, which was also an exercise in exerting his authority. Encouraged by his agent, Major Mahon upped the ante with the 'combination' and in January 1847 consented to:

> proceed against those that are known to have the means to pay at least a part ... so to any remarks that the Roscommon Journal may make, I heed them not ... we are not doing any tyrannical or cruel and making those pay their rent or give up their land, who are known to refuse doing so from combination is but an act of justice to those who pay & are willing to do so without putting us to trouble.[28]

Ross Mahon did not need reminding: in his opinion the improvement of the estate could not be brought about until 'the land is cleared of at least two thirds of the population'.[29] While he has traditionally been portrayed as the villain in the Strokestown Famine narrative, the correspondence between the pair fully implicates Major Denis Mahon in all of the decision-making that was to take place in 1847. Indeed, within weeks of Ross Mahon's appointment, his employer wrote that 'I shall feel obliged by your submitting them [eviction plans] for my approval prior to their being carried into execution'.[30] Ross Mahon's plans were a little more extreme than the landlord's, believing that about £24,000 should be spent on emigration, ridding the estate in the process of 1,600 families (over 8,000 people), as there was 'no rent paying that I hear among the lower class of tenants'.[31] But before capital was invested in emigrating tenants, Major Denis Mahon wished to know 'whether they have in the first instance got rid of their under-tenants, as I consider it hard on me to send out people who not only owe me rent but also leave me a parcel of pauper under-tenants'.[32] With this ascertained, a scheme of assisted emigration was put into place, albeit on a smaller scale than that planned by the agent.

Ross Mahon began his tenure at Strokestown without any animosity. In November 1846 he organized to have the Dublin firm of Brassington and Gale, land surveyors,

As agent, John Ross Mahon began to pay close attention to those who, despite being in a position to do so, had not paid their rent in a number of years. These people, it was claimed, were making the most of the 'bad times', as this distress notice from the parish of Bumlin, near Strokestown, in 1848 showed.

walk over the estate, map and value it. As a result of this survey, and due to the severity of winter, he consented to grant a reduction to tenants on any lands that were overset and overvalued. But by early 1847 the undertaking of an estate census was seen as an intrusion on an already hard-pressed tenantry, and as a change in estate

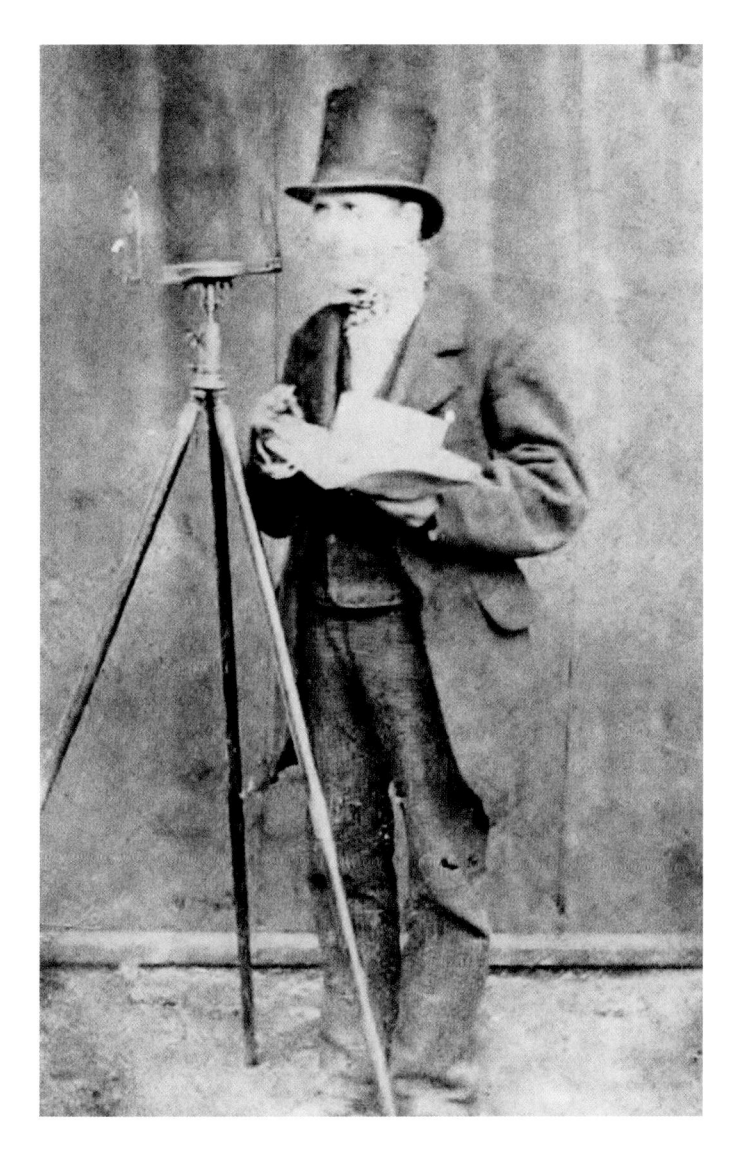

Edward Murphy (1808–94) was a school teacher and an engineer on the public works scheme near Strokestown during the Great Famine. To be given work on the public works, the poor had to prove that they were destitute.

policy. On 21 March 1847, the census was delivered to Major Denis Mahon. Recording the townland, parish, family and number of persons living on the estate, the census was to provide the genesis for the assisted emigration scheme that would make both Strokestown and the Mahons notorious.[33] Although the 1845 estate rental had listed the names of 745 lessees, or direct rent payers, Ross Mahon found a mostly impoverished population of 11,958 people. On closer examination of the tenants it was also found that several were taking advantage of the potato failure 'in order to allow them carry out their combination not to pay any rent'.[34] It was decided that

As distress worsened, tenants in arrears and those 'unlikely to recover themselves' were offered compensation for surrendering their house and land, as the cases of William Fallon and Elizabeth Farrell (shown above) reveal.

those who were in arrears prior to 1845 were not to be given any lenience, as 1846 had been the only 'bad year'. Appalled by the census findings Ross Mahon reported to his employer that:

> I think the facts are sufficient without any further remarks of mine to show the impossibility of collecting poor rates or of effecting any change in the condition of the people while the land remains in such small divisions in the hands of paupers unable to support themselves much less to till it to advantage.[35]

He further warned:

> I am convinced unless the greater part of the population are removed from your estate, the poor rates of this electoral division will exceed the receipts of rent, and the division being almost entirely your property, the greater part of the poor rate must fall upon you.[36]

His thinking was simple. Overpopulation and overcrowding were too great and the estate could not afford either to keep people in the workhouse or to compensate

In the majority of cases at Strokestown it was women who queued to be given relief. They had to supply their name, address and details of the person who recommended them for assistance.

The Cencus As on Major Mahons Estate Strokestown Rent=Office 21 March 1847

Townlands	Parish	Families	No. of Persons or Individuals
1 Aughadangan	Lissonuffy	19	91
2 Aughaclogher	Cloonfinlough	1	7
3 Ballinafad	Cloonfinlough	45	216
4 Bavally	Kilglas	14	73
5 Bumlin	Bumlin	3	24
6 Ballyhobert	Lissonuffy	40	242
7 Ballintober (Ballyhammon)	Ballintober	13	101
8 Belcagh	Aughrim	36	200
9 Carton	Kilmore	39	211
10 Curtowna	Lissonuffy	21	117
11 Curries (Corry)	Aughrim	145	662
12 Cloonfad	do	56	339

In order to bring the estate to order, in late 1846 Major Denis Mahon carried out a census of the estate. Delivered to him in March 1847, the census confirmed the problem of gross overcrowding and subdivision of the land. Although his rent books listed only 745 leaseholders, the census confirmed that there were 11,958 people living on the estate.

In most cases tenants were given little more than a month to prepare for emig... and were provided with temporary outdoor relief, indicating that the le... of their houses commenced at once. Coinciding with the assisted emig... scheme those who had not been chosen were also encouraged to take compensation...

4

'Orphaned to the World': Assisted Emigration in Practice

As the census and emigration lists were being compiled, tenants learned of their fate. Initially, it was hoped that the emigration scheme would include the greatest number of tenants possible, but having failed to secure ready finance for the project, the plan was scaled back somewhat to include only a 'limited number'.[1] Tenants were selected from thirty-two townlands and in most cases offered some 'lucrative' enticement to go, although no inducement could persuade some of them, such as John Egan and James Duffy of Cregga. These 'lucrative offers' included granting compensation for seed potatoes, for throwing down their houses and for giving up their crop. In most cases tenants were given little more than a month to prepare for emigration and were provided with temporary outdoor relief, indicating that the levelling of their houses commenced at once. Coinciding with the assisted emigration scheme, those who had not been chosen were also encouraged to take compensation and emigrate at their own expense. They included Winny Brennan of Cloonraine who was given one pound to surrender her holding and Peter McGlynn who was given compensation for a cow and a calf. Mrs Carley, the coachman's wife at Strokestown House, was given a gratuity on going to America. For these and many others, the message was simple. They could 'go where you like' upon surrendering possession of their holdings.[2] Those deemed too old to emigrate were also compensated, as were orphans who were also 'encouraged' to go.[3] Some stayed in the sanguine hope

> that Lord Palmerston is doing so, and that he states his plan for the Emigration of his Tenantry in Co Sligo, goes on very well — do you know his Agent? would you consider it advisable to communicate with him on the Subject? I regret to say I shall not be able to go over so soon as I had intended I have got a very severe Cold, which will take me some

John Ross Mahon had enquired into how other assisted emigration schemes had operated, particularly the one on Lord Palmerston's estate in county Sligo, as this letter shows.

that they would be entrusted with the holdings of their neighbours who emigrated. Such decisions suited the landlord who hoped that remittances would be sent home to Strokestown and so the rent of those who remained would be paid. For tenants who were allowed to remain, adherence to strict guidelines was a necessity; a tenant named Lynam was told 'to get rid of paupers on his holding and build good slated houses from house to archway' before his lease would be renewed.[4] As an inducement to get rid of some of the more troublesome tenants, and those who possessed no means for self-advancement, Major Denis Mahon allowed them to remove the crop

For John Ross Mahon, an assisted emigration scheme made perfect economic sense. Removing the responsibility of providing for these tenants whether on the estate or in the workhouse would allow those who remained a chance to recover, as indicated in this memorandum compiled in defence of the emigration scheme.

that had been planted: 'I quite agree with you that it will be very advantageous to get rid of the pauper tenants … by giving crops as you propose'.[5]

In early May final arrangements were made with J. & W. Robinson, a shipping firm in Liverpool, for the passage of 800 'statue adults' to Quebec at £3 2s. 6d. each, plus children under fourteen who went at half price.[6] In total 275 families, containing 1,490 people, were included.[7] Initially, there was little opposition to the emigration scheme and the levelling of houses.[8] Crops, animals and household possessions were snapped up at auctions and fair days, and those who remained were delighted to acquire them. These people would later clamour to be given whatever land was to be re-divided. Initially, Major Denis Mahon was praised for his benevolence and 'liberality in sending nearly 300 families to Quebec' and covering the costs of the trip.[9] However, it wasn't long before condemnation followed in local, provincial and national newspapers. In

July, the *Roscommon Journal* was particularly critical of the clearance of the tenants at Strokestown, noting that:

> Our prisons will be kept crowded; our poorhouse will be kept full; and our streets will be inundated by this 'clearance system' — this new mode of depopulating.[10]

One of the most enduring images of the Great Famine remains that of the coffin ship on which ill-fated paupers travelled to places such as the Americas or Australia, dying in large numbers in the process. Sir Stephen de Vere, the son of a prominent county Limerick landlord, was among the first to highlight the appalling conditions that these emigrants faced.[11] The Mahon tenants who travelled to British North America (Canada) in 1847 were among the first to be described as travelling on coffin ships.

The Mahon tenants were escorted to Liverpool by the bailiff, John Robinson, who was instructed to wait until the last of the tenants had emigrated. On his return to Strokestown in late May, he informed Major Denis Mahon that everything had gone smoothly.

Coinciding with the assisted emigration scheme those who had not been [selected?] were also encouraged to take compensation and emigrate at their own expense.

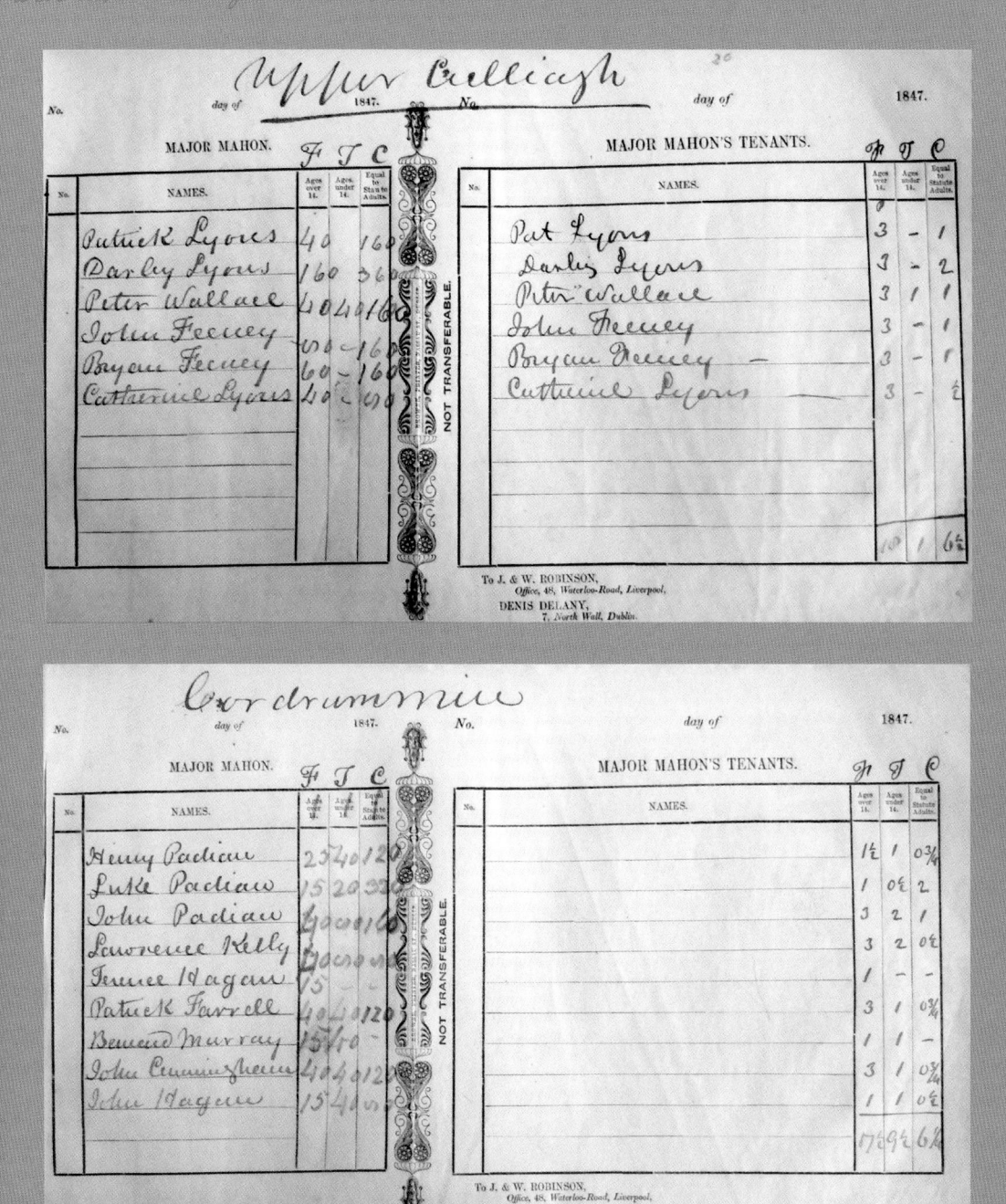

Tenants from the townland of Upper Culliagh and Cordrummin who were assisted in emigrating in 1847 included the Lyons, Wallace, Feeney, Padian, Hagan, Kelly, Murray, Farrell and Cunningham families.

ASSISTED EMIGRATION IN PRACTICE   69

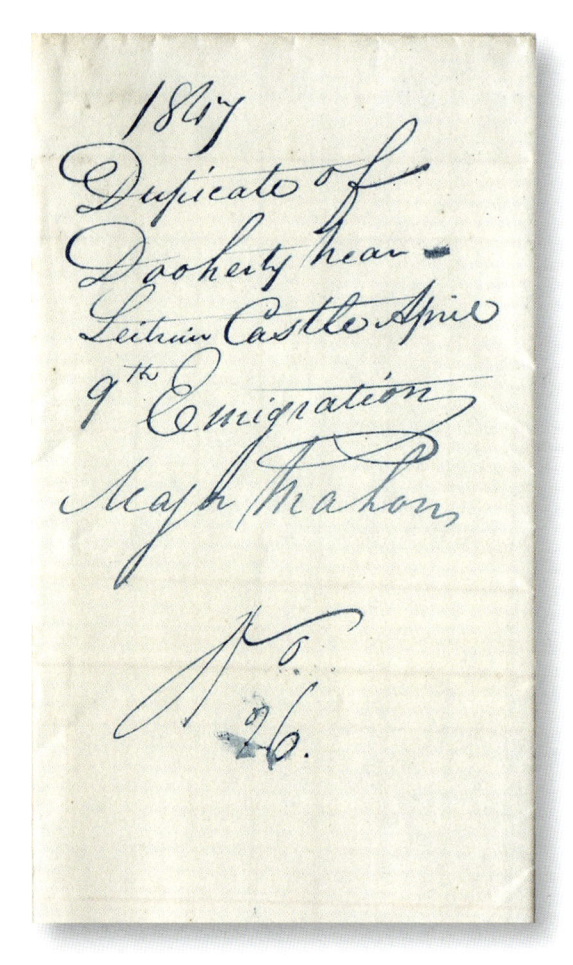

Public opinion began to change in September 1847 when word filtered back to the local community that many of the emigrants had died en route to Canada. There was also displeasure at the continued removal of tenants. When ejectment notices were served on the townland of Dooherty, Major Mahon's fate was sealed.

By the time they reached Grosse Île, a quarantine station on the St Lawrence River outside the city of Quebec, almost half of the tenants were dead or dying. The ships on which they travelled would soon gain notoriety for the disease, sickness and death that prevailed on them. Thousands had already perished on the crossing to British North America, perhaps as many as 6,000 in 1847 alone.[12]

Although Major Denis Mahon had ensured that his tenants would receive more than the standard rations for such voyages (departing tenants were supplied with more than the government rations and included a weekly distribution of 6lbs of sugar, 10oz of tea, coffee, 8lbs of rice, 14lbs of oatmeal, one dozen herrings, 1.5lbs of soap, 1 pint of vinegar, pepper and salt), many were simply unfit for the voyage across the Atlantic Ocean. For many, the ample provisions mattered little as they were already severely sick long before their departure from Roscommon. The six members of the Saunders family of Tooreen, for example, were all noted to be 'sick with fever' when the selection process was carried out in late March. In a number of instances several family members were unable to leave owing to illness. Accompanying the tenants to Liverpool was the bailiff, John Robinson, who was instructed to make sure that all of the 1,490 emigrants departed. When he returned to his duties at Strokestown, Robinson was happy to report to Major Denis Mahon that everything had gone according to plan. Little did he, or indeed anyone connected with Strokestown, realize the fate that lay before the

> In addition to the sums given as gratuities to the poorer class of these Tenants who were dispossessed, they were permitted to take away their crops, without being charged any rent. Such as were able to pay were charged a year's rent of the ground *on which the crop stood*, calculated at the average acreable rent of their holdings.
>
> On the Townland of CORDRUMMIN the Tenants evicted were paid full remuneration for the seed and labour, which amounted to the full value of their crop; and in no instance was any Tenant deprived of the crop, although by law it became Major Mahon's on the Sheriff giving possession of the land.
>
> As an instance of the anxiety of the Tenants to emigrate it may be remarked, that on the Townland of KILMACK-NANNY, where but five ejectments were served, thirty-three families emigrated, not one of whom was under ejectment: also twenty-six from TULLY, in addition to those from SCRAMOGUE and GRAFFOGUE.
>
> It has been calculated that a sum of £4000 will be required for putting the lands in a fit state for setting; which is a very low estimate, in consequence of their present impoverished condition, and the number of bad and useless fences and subdivisions on them. It is intended to divide these farms in a manner suitable to the introduction of a Rotation System of improved husbandry, hitherto totally unknown on this Estate.
>
> The object of giving the area and Ordnance valuation of each Townland, is to show the relative letting of these lands of which Major Mahon got possession. It will appear that the yearly rent of all these Townlands is scarcely more than the Ordnance valuation, with £25 per cent. added, which is considered to be the letting value.

John Ross Mahon staunchly defended the emigration scheme, highlighting that tenants were compensated for crops, animals and other materials and that they had been given more than the government allowance for their passage.

emigrants. Holed up in Liverpool docks for two days, the tenants waited to leave onboard four ships – the *Virginius, John Munn, Erin's Queen* and *Naomi*.[13] With cholera and typhus rampant, the Mahon tenants were exposed to the ravages of disease. The first of the Mahon tenants arrived at Grosse Île on 17 July onboard the *Erin's Queen* but were detained for more than twelve days in quarantine. By the end of the month they were joined by the emigrants from the *Virginius*, which had spent more than 63 days at sea.[14] Within days the *John Munn* and the *Naomi* would arrive carrying even more dead. The *Toronto Globe* newspaper was among the first to highlight the problems encountered by the passengers on board the *Virginius* and thus reported its arrival at Grosse Île:

> The *Virginius* from Liverpool, with 496 passengers, had lost 158 by death, nearly one third of the whole, and she had 180 sick; above one half the whole will never see their home in the new world.[15]

Those who managed to emerge from the ship were described as 'ghastly, yellow-looking spectres, unshaven and hollow cheeked'.[16] Dr George Douglas, who treated and spoke with the Mahon tenants at Grosse Île, noted that some had died before

Assisted emigration

It is estimated that as many as 80,000 people were assisted in emigrating during the Great Famine. These people had their passage paid by the British government, landlords, Poor Law Unions and philanthropists. Landlord-assisted schemes included those of Charles Wandesforde (Kilkenny), the 3rd marquis of Lansdowne (Kerry) and the 5th Earl Fitzwilliam (Wicklow). The fate of these emigrants varied greatly. The Wandesforde and Fitzwilliam tenants were sent to Pennsylvania and New Brunswick respectively, where they found ready employment. In contrast, Lansdowne's tenants settled in abject poverty in the notorious Five Points district of New York.

Emigrants were to be found in all parts of the world – the US, Australia, Britain, Canada, South America and South Africa. This latter destination has largely been overlooked because the numbers involved were so small, just over 5,000. Attitudes towards the emigrant Irish played a significant role in keeping these numbers low. In 1849, following plans to establish a penal colony in South Africa's Western Cape, the residents of Cape Town refused to let a convict ship, *Neptune*, land. With almost 300 passengers on board, including the Young Irelander, John Mitchel, the ship lay at anchor for over five months off the coast of Cape Town. Known as the 'Anti-Convict' protest, those who tried to supply the ship with provisions were boycotted and put out of business.

departing Liverpool.[17] The condition of the *Virginius* passengers eventually brought about an outcry from the British North American officials and prompted a government investigation.[18] It was also claimed that on arrival at Grosse Île the ship's master had to bribe his crew, at the rate of a sovereign per corpse, to remove the dead from the hold. On the ship *Erin's Queen*, the situation was no better: 78 passengers had died and a further 104 were sick. Again, according to the *Globe*, 'the filth and dirt in these vessels hold creates such an effluvium as to make it difficult to breathe'.[19] While in harbour the ship was abandoned by the crew and captain who feared for their lives.[20] On the ship *John Munn* more than 100 were sick and 59 were dead, while on the *Naomi* 78 were dead. The horrendous conditions on board the ships were later relayed to a grandson of Daniel Tighe. Daniel had travelled on the *Naomi* with his family:

> The voyage was a long nightmare of eight weeks. Drinking water ran low and food was reduced to one meal a day. Comfort and hygiene were non-existent. Typhus broke out on board, and the ship was ordered to stop at Grosse Île. Of Mary Tighe's family only two children survived: Daniel, aged 12 and Catherine, 9 years old. When the children left the ship, they never saw the other family members again, nor did they have any word about them.[21]

The final death toll of the Mahon emigrants was staggering: of the 1,490 who had left Strokestown over 700 died, and were buried at sea or on Grosse Île. Some lingered for weeks at the quarantine stations before succumbing to a variety of diseases. On the *John Munn* the Strokestown dead included William Holmes, Patrick McGuire and Nancy Tighe. Mahon tenants who died on board the *Naomi* included Patrick Brennan, aged 3; three members of the Cox family, Patrick, Dolly and Thomas; Luke Fallon, aged 1; Hannah McDermott, aged 2 and Mary McGuire, aged 3. The plight of the Murray family of Gurtoose was particularly poignant. The dead included three generations: Luke, aged 70; Ann, aged 50 and John, aged 3. Another of the family, Luke, aged 8, survived the passage but died six days later at the Hospital de la Grosse Île.[22]

Moreover, a significant number (perhaps more than sixty) of the Strokestown emigrants were orphaned on Canadian shores and were initially cared for by La Société charitable des Dames Catholiques de Québec.[23] They were subsequently

Realizing that they had overcharged Major Mahon for the emigration scheme, the firm J. & W. Robinson reimbursed the estate. This money was used to send others to America.

adopted through the generosity of the Catholic Church and French-Canadian families. These orphans included Patrick Madden, aged 17, and his sister Maria, aged 11, who arrived at the Quebec City orphanage on 18 August, their parents having perished on the crossing onboard the *Virginius*.[24] Others included Bridget Egan, aged 6, and her brother Peter, aged 16, from Kilglass, adopted by the Belanger family of Rimouski; Catherine Feeney, aged 18, and her sister Anne, aged 8, from Bumlin, adopted by a Mr Kelly of St Sylvester, and Patrick and Thomas Quinn from Lissonuffy, who were placed in the care of George Bourque in Nicolet, south-west of Quebec City. Both the Quinns would later become priests.[25] The story of the Tighes epitomized the experience of these Famine orphans:

> On 8 August 1847 Daniel and Catherine along with several other immigrants left Grosse Île on a sail boat which brought them to Quebec ... Mr and Mrs Coulombe adopted Daniel and decided to keep Catherine for a few days while waiting for a house to welcome her. The children cried so hard at the idea of being separated that they were inconsolable. In the end they kept them both.[26]

Tenants from the townlands of Aughadangan and Dooherty who were assisted in emigrating in 1847 included the Brannon, Donaghue, Duffy, Dwyer, Hunt, Tighe and Salts families.

ASSISTED EMIGRATION IN PRACTICE

By the end of August though, relations between landlord and tenants were deteriorating rapidly. Moreover, once-cordial relations between Major Denis Mahon and the Revd Michael McDermott, parish priest of Strokestown, were irrevocably strained. The fallout was to hav

5

Targeting the 'Snug' Tenantry: Prelude to Murder

> It is not a matter of surprise to see on a morning twenty dead bodies thrown across the backs of asses, rolled up in mats, or in the squalid rags in which they had died, going to the graveyard, while one single coffin could not be procured by their friends.[1]

The summer months of 1847 were relatively calm at Strokestown and there does not appear to have been any immediate backlash against the assisted emigration scheme or the continued clearances. By the end of August though, relations between landlord and tenants were deteriorating rapidly.[2] Moreover, once-cordial relations between Major Denis Mahon and the Revd Michael McDermott, parish priest of Strokestown, were irrevocably strained. The fallout was to have an immediate and lasting effect on the people of Roscommon. Although the facts surrounding the murder of Major Denis Mahon have been examined by a number of historians to date, it is necessary nonetheless to recount them briefly here. The murder plan had been hatched in several locations, but in the townlands of Dooherty, Leitrim and Carnalasson there was particular antipathy towards Mahon for the eviction notices that were served in early Autumn 1847.

On 2 November 1847, as he returned from a meeting of the Roscommon Board of Guardians, where, ironically, he had gone to seek relief for his tenants, Major Denis Mahon was shot dead near the townland of Dooherty, an area quickly dubbed the 'Khyber pass'.[3] Mahon's murder was the most high-profile assassination of the Famine

Although the potato crop had not entirely failed in 1847, extreme scarcity was experienced as many had not planted a crop in the first place. Matters worsened towards the end of the summer when the government decided to stop the soup kitchens and to scale back the public works.

period[4] and the political fallout from the murder made it the most sensational. Within days, the murder came to define the misgovernment of Ireland and the event was being discussed across the world. What followed was a long period of debate, accusation and controversy largely played out on religious grounds. Strokestown became synonymous with eviction, and heated exchanges occurred in the House of Commons and in the provincial, national and international press.

For Major Denis Mahon, the assisted emigration scheme was only the beginning of the plan to bring the estate to order. He later expressed disappointment, contrary to his earlier statement, that he had not received any large holdings during the emigration scheme, another indication that it had been the poorest, those of the 'worst description', who had been assisted.[5] The removal of almost 1,500 people and the departure of many more heralded a change in the estate's leasing policy. Going forward tenants in town plots were to be given yearly leases, meaning that they could be disposed of easily, or their rent increased without recourse to the law.

Concerned about the future, some, such as Margaret Brice and Peter Casey, decided to surrender their holdings and take the compensation being offered to them.

Rental of the Estate of Strokestown for Half[...]

No.	DENOMINATIONS.		TENANTS.	Rent when due Charge	Arrears. Rent & Rent Charge	Half Year Rent. Rent Charge
				69 / : 3	204 / 5½	2093 0
255	Tambeg	912	Henry Holden	" 2 : 4	2 19 4	3 19
256	do	792	James Hennegan	" " 7		1 7
257	do	790	John Geagherty	" " 7		1 17
258	do	x	Patt Maguire Hatter	" " 9	" 16 3	" 13
259	do	795	Peter Cleary	" 9 . 7		12 1
260	do	799	John Higgins	" 1 : 12		1 0
261	do	792	John Igoe	" " "		" 13
262	do	792	Michael Kelly	" 5 : 1		6 6
263	do	903	John Maguire	" 2 : 5		3 13
264	do		Bailie Mahon Esquire	" 3 : 0		3 10
265	do	792	John Holden	" 1 : 11		6 0
266	do	903	Major Mahon	" 4 : 7	9 11 4½	6 3
267	do		Major Mahon	" 4 . 7		6 3

It was a move that was to further alienate Major Mahon from the tenantry.[6] In these challenging times he now decided that he should be 'on the spot and at all times'.[7] Crucially, the emigration scheme also coincided with the government decision to end the soup kitchens and to scale back the public works. As landlord, the burden of providing relief once again became Major Denis Mahon's responsibility and so he set about revising the relief lists at the end of August. This action, as we shall see below, was much to the displeasure of the Revd Michael McDermott, who believed it to be a slight on his character. To further avoid providing for these people, more than 1,900 civil bills for eviction were entered at the Strokestown petty sessions. By late summer Major Denis Mahon began focusing on those who had heretofore escaped the attention of agent and bailiff alike. Hoping that he would be in a position to get in rents from 'the better class' of tenants, particular attention was focussed on the middleman, Patrick Browne of Cloonfad, who had been given 'plenty of indulgence'.[8]

Particularly vexing to Major Denis Mahon was the number of tenants who he described as 'snug' and who refused to pay their rent. It was this group that he targeted in 1847. The document here shows the accounts for the townland of Farnbeg in 1842, which was in arrears. By 1847 some of these tenants refused to pay rent although many were in a position to do so.

This was significant and the eviction of Browne and his under-tenants was one that came back to haunt the Mahons, and the estate in general.[9] Another group that received particular attention were those perceived to be 'snug people', principally the Castlenode tenants. According to the landlord: 'I would have thought with that class of people it would have been ample indulgence to have "forgiven the rent due" and let them find their own way out'.[10] Elsewhere, Major Denis Mahon was determined 'to get out of the hands of so bad a set of & such a nest of paupers', those who were 'not improving' and 'badly off'.[11] From September to November 1847 perhaps as many as 1,000 people were evicted. Reflecting the devastation caused by eviction, fever sheds

TARGETING THE 'SNUG' TENANTRY: PRELUDE TO MURDER   83

The failure of the potato crop in 1848 was a severe blow to those who had survived until this point. Such was the case for the Ballinafad tenants who petitioned for help; their 'hopes were blinded' by yet another failure. These once-prosperous tenants were now on the verge of ruin.

and temporary housing sprung up throughout the estate.[12] Strokestown now had the appearance of a slum. 'Fever, famine and dysentery' were said to prevail in conditions exacerbated by the landlords who were 'acting their part in this tragic scene'.[13]

When the number of fatalities onboard the Quebec-bound ships became known, Major Mahon's fate was effectively sealed. John Ross Mahon was informed that a plot 'by persons in comfortable circumstances' had been organized to shoot his employer and emigrants in America had provided the money to do so.[14] Evidently, Major Mahon took the threat seriously and he decided to carry a gun with him on all occasions.[15] The final straw for tenants came in early October 1847 when Major Denis Mahon decided to remove refractory tenants from the townlands of Dooherty, Leitrim and Cornashina.[16] Dooherty, in particular, was a prized possession and even before Mahon had ordered that tenants were to be removed, there were several 'strong' farmers

From Old World to New

Michael Calhoun Dufficy was born near Strokestown in 1839 in the months that followed 'The Night of the Big Wind'. The Dufficy family farmed a little more than a quarter acre of land on the eve of the Famine, and were among those who were affected most by the arrival of potato blight. Leaving Ireland in late 1846, as the second crop of potatoes failed and the realization dawned that famine would not be short lived, the Dufficys travelled to America. Settling initially in New Orleans, within two years of their arrival, Francis Dufficy, head of the family, was dead and so the remainder of the family went to California. Having been schooled in New Orleans, Michael Calhoun Dufficy was imbued with an entrepreneurial zeal and after an initial period farming in Yuba County he undertook a number of business ventures including a merchandising store in Marysville from 1854 to 1876; the Western Hotel; the St Nicholas Hotel and later the Brooklyn Hotel in San Francisco. In Marysville and San Rafael, he acted as a notary public and in later life also filled the office of justice of the peace. By 1905 he was listed among the 'notable people of California' and was described as 'a gentleman of culture'.

watching for their chance to rent it.[17] Although controversy still reigns as to the precise location of Mahon's murder, it is certain that his decision to target the townland of Dooherty led to his demise.[18]

In those final months, life carried on as normal for Major Denis Mahon. Strokestown, like so many other country houses, could be best described as a house of plenty in a time of want. Despite the indebted nature of the estate, the annual expenditure of the house remained over £3,000 and until he initiated his plan of assisted emigration, Mahon's only financial pressure was to meet the interest on loans and to pay jointures.[19] In addition, he spent long periods in London, where his leisure pursuits included attending the theatre and socializing in the city's fashionable gentry clubs. Back at Strokestown he enjoyed shooting and hunting, regularly playing host to guests such as Lord Clonbrock, Lord Lorton and other neighbouring gentry.[20] Guests at Strokestown throughout the Famine continued to be entertained and sumptuously fed.[21]

Wine and champagne were shipped from Southampton along with other luxury goods, while instructions were given to the gamekeepers on how a 'good buck' should be shot; 'do not move the deer much previously or ride after them in which case the venison will not keep'.[22] No expense was spared for the visits of family members and to make the estate look aesthetically pleasing for visitors.[23] The Mahons, however,

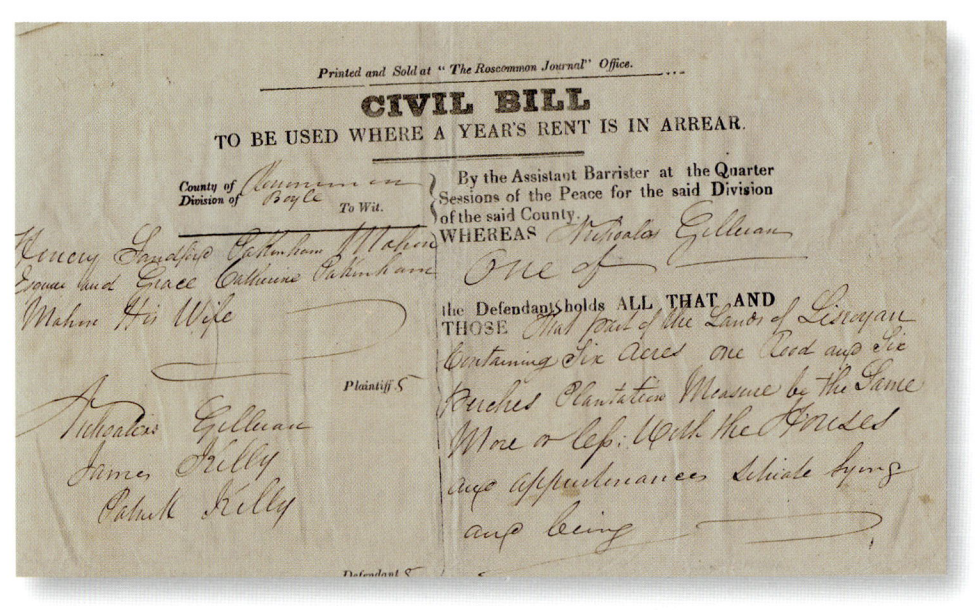

Across the Strokestown estate, the dreaded Civil Bill issued for arrears of rent became an all-too-common occurrence. Although given a stay of execution before final removal, in most cases upwards of six months, tenants knew that ultimately eviction would be their lot.

The opulence of the 'Big House' was in stark contrast to the experience of the Strokestown tenantry. Wine and champagne characterized the life of the Mahon family in 1847 as they celebrated the marriage of Grace Catherine in March of that year.

Amid continued hunger in Roscommon, venison was sent on a weekly basis to Boyle Barracks.

were not the only people who continued to spend during the Famine and the local expenditure of money is interesting. The Kiltrustan church, near Strokestown, was built during the Famine years, and the parish priest was praised for his indefatigable exertions in this period.[24] In September 1848 a congregation of priests and bishops met at Strokestown for three days, and there was said to have been great feasting and celebration. In the parish of Kilglass where hundreds had been evicted, the Revd Henry Brennan accumulated a large debt in the building of a new church.[25] Also, the various political parties spent heavily in the lead up to the 1847 general election, which was said to have been 'hotly contested' in county Roscommon.[26]

By now the ravages of the Famine in Roscommon were all too apparent. The Revd Boyd's description of the locality left little to the imagination:

> My heart sickens at the sight of the multitude of wretches who swarm in these ill-fated villages of Slieve Bawn without food or employment or a prospect of either and who have not a perch of tillage on the earth. Death by starvation stares them in the face, and they already speak the language of despair.[27]

The Strokestown relief committee, who had laboured to provide for the poor of the locality, had exhausted resources and were now 'only able to distribute a small quantity of bread and soup ... and when we had done we could not promise the poor starved wretches any further assistance'.[28] Emigration remained the only viable solution in the minds of many, including formerly prosperous tenants. Those who had not been selected in assisted emigration now looked to be included on any other scheme that might come to pass. While they waited they acted with some degree of optimism and planted a crop of potatoes.[29] Their condition differed greatly from that of the Mahons, who in early March 1847 travelled to London for the celebration of the marriage of Grace Mahon and Henry Sandford Pakenham, son of the Revd Henry Pakenham, Dean of St Patrick's and Christchurch Cathedral, Dublin.[30] Sojourning through France and Italy, the newly married couple spent the summer months oblivious to the conditions in Roscommon and the impending disaster that assisted emigration would bring.[31] Then aged twenty-four, Pakenham hardly expected that within eight months of his wedding he would be the owner of Strokestown.

By the end of the summer of 1847 there was growing resentment towards Major Denis Mahon and his team of officials.

TARGETING THE 'SNUG' TENANTRY: PRELUDE TO MURDER

> a letter yesterday —
> McGuire written hereabouts — "Do as you
> please but mark the consequence of turning off
> your herd — & you need not think that the country
> is so beat yet as that they will listen to you, to
> put away a man that is minding his business
> better than them theives telling you the stories of him
> & watch them & you find out who is doing badness to
> you & Let her know that you may be taken oftentimes
> before & if you do, you may keep the house for I
> am the man that will watch you day & night If
> you dont change your mind
>
> Molly McGuire
>
> and here is the Doctor
>
> that is your bed
>
> It is nothing I say but what I will
> stand firm to By God
> dont talk of this G—

Other members of the estate administration, including Thomas Roberts, the sub-agent, were threatened by secret societies like the Molly Maguires that they would meet the same fate as Major Mahon.

Matters came to a head at a meeting of the Strokestown relief committee at the end of August. On his return and having looked over the committee books, Major Denis Mahon questioned why the members had not met since 24 July. Clearly annoyed at the accusation of the

6

'Worse than Cromwell and Yet He Lives': the Murder of Major Mahon

{ Within one hour of the foul deed being perpetrated the several hills were lighted by bonfires in every direction.[1] }

Throughout the summer of 1847, Major Denis Mahon had played a limited role in the administration of the Strokestown relief committee, which naturally drew criticism from the Revd Michael McDermott and others. There was further criticism of the Mahon family for their having spent much of the year in London, where it was suggested they were ignoring the plight of their tenants. In their absence the relief committee didn't meet for a five-week period in July and August. This failure to meet was striking because of the devastation that was taking hold locally, the extent of which was aptly captured by the editor of the *Roscommon Journal* who noted that 'the people must die in numbers unless relieved'.[2] Matters came to a head at a meeting of the Strokestown relief committee at the end of August. On his return and having looked over the committee books, Major Denis Mahon questioned why the members had not met since 24 July. Clearly annoyed at the accusation of them failing in their duties, the Revd McDermott assured him that everything was in order and there was no need for them to have met. When Mahon questioned the clerk, Charles Costello, about the vouchers and those receiving relief, the priest proceeded to abuse him, calling Mahon a 'stupid ass' and inquiring if he had ever received any schooling.

ANOTHER DREADFUL MURDER.

STROKESTOWN, TUESDAY NIGHT.—As Major Mahon was returning home from a meeting of the board of guardians of Roscommon union, on this evening, he was *shot dead* by an assassin, about four miles from Strokestown. The melancholy occurrence took place about twenty minutes past six o'clock in the evening. Major Mahon has been in possession of the Hartland property for a couple of years. The tenants owed three years' rent, amounting to thirty thousand pounds. At first, the tenants refused to pay rent, till the land, or give it up. Last year, however, a large portion of them agreed to leave the country; and Major Mahon, at his own expense, chartered two vessels, and sent a number of the tenantry to America. Long, however, before this occurred, it was well known in the country that Major Mahon was a doomed man. His name stood first upon the list of twelve gentlemen, all of whom have been doomed to death on account of their refusal to continue the conacre system. The failure of the potato crop saved them for a time. As Major Mahon has been taken off, there is little doubt that other gentlemen will soon follow. Major Mahon, within the last few days, was publicly denounced, in one of the reports to head quarters, as an absentee, and one who refused to contribute to the local subscription of the neighbourhood.—*Correspondent of the Evening Mail.*

The murder of Major Mahon became an international news sensation. It was arguably the most high-profile murder of the Great Irish Famine (*Belfast Newsletter*, 5 Nov. 1847).

'Here have I been for two hours trying to drive into his stupid head some information and he is so ignorant he cannot understand it' thundered the cleric. This outburst finished with him accusing Major Denis Mahon of having amused himself in London and of burning and leveling houses on his return. Some days later Major Mahon wrote to McDermott seeking him to withdraw his claims:

Sir, the very unwarrantable language which you made use of towards me on Saturday, the 28th inst, at a meeting of the relief committee, in the presence of Dr Shanley and others, and further if I am rightly informed, repeated again by you at your chapels the following Sunday – in justice to my own feelings, and as landlord over a numerous tenantry, I feel doubly called upon to request you will give me an opportunity of replying to your very serious charges. As I understand the relief committee are to meet on Friday next, I request you will come prepared to prove them, as I am determined to lay the matter before the committee on that day [or whatever day they shall meet], and submit to them how far you were warranted in making such charges against me.[3]

McDermott was not for turning, informing Mahon that:

> Until you make atonement to my feelings as a clergyman, for your insolent and personal attacks, I shall attend no meeting where you are present, either publicly or privately. I make this reply to convince you that I am only anxious to avoid a person whose conduct seems so extraordinary, and who seems to disregard the ordinary forms of civil society. My calling does not allow me to resent the insults I receive, and therefore common prudence, as well as religion, points out to me the necessity of withdrawing myself from the society of persons who may be inclined to offend me.[4]

They were both stubborn characters and neither was prepared to give an inch. McDermott, a post-emancipation clergyman, like his counterparts elsewhere, was determined to put his stamp of authority on the local population. Having only assumed ownership of the estate officially in 1845, Major Mahon was determined to take back the town that his family had controlled since the 1660s. These outbursts, although trivial and petty, are crucial in understanding events in Strokestown in 1847 and later.[5]

In the past McDermott had displayed deference to the landlord on all occasions. Indeed, in 1836, for example, he had warmly greeted Major Mahon's arrival in Strokestown:

> I beg to assure you of my sincere gratitude for your kindness towards myself personally, and your encouragement to the improvements and industrious habits of my parishioners since you came to reside amongst us. May god almighty render to you the full reward of your good intentions, and grant you long life to reap the fruit of your kindly disposition in the affections of the poor tenantry.[6]

In the days after the murder, members of the Roscommon gentry met to put on record their abhorrence of the deed. The resolution of the meeting called on the public to provide information to help apprehend the assassins.

A further letter, dated July 1845, reminded Major Denis Mahon of his loyalty: 'I always use my utmost exertions to promote peace among the people and above all respect and punctuality to their landlords and the proprietors of the soil'.[7] But the seeds of McDermott's annoyance stemmed from Mahon's appointment of the 'most odious and obnoxious characters' as overseers of the local public works scheme.[8] This ill-will was indicative of the petty squabbling that existed throughout the country with regard to local relief. A staunch Repealer, the Revd McDermott was also a member of the Catholic Defence Association and regularly came to the aid of tenants threatened

FM 8-9

Strokestown March 17 1848

My dear Sir

I am happy to say that we have in custody two men named Hester & Gardner who are deeply implicated in the murder — Hester was servant boy to Hasty who was arrested some time since — and his information exactly agrees with that of Rigney who had been employed by Hasty to follow Major Mahon on the occasion of his going to Roscommon to attend the election of a Doctor for the Infirmary — Gardner is ill or pretends to be so & has not told any thing — We find we can put no

The hunt for those responsible for the murder continued into 1848, with the police travelling to Britain and Canada to apprehend suspects. Here, John Ross Mahon describes the arrest of two men named Hester and Gardiner in March 1848.

(*Top*) Although it was the unwritten rule of mid-nineteenth-century Ireland not to give information about secret societies, a number of tenants came forward. For their efforts they were placed in protective custody before being assisted in emigrating. This document shows assistance given to the Rigney and Brennan families for information relating to the murder.

(*Left*) According to the social memory of the Famine, those charged with involvement in the murder of Major Mahon were innocent and the real culprits evaded arrest. In August 1848, Patrick Hasty was hanged in Roscommon town for his alleged part in the conspiracy.

96   STROKESTOWN AND THE GREAT IRISH FAMINE

> Doorty, 23rd 1848
> Dear Pat we did not get protection as yet nor any one to look after us and we are in dread of our lives every night and day not now but we will be killed or distroyd in the morning after the night and also we were Dan and but of the Male so we do not know what we will do J was speaking Saterday last to the Honourable Martin French and he said he received two letters on that count and said he could do nothing on till the peter McTeay would come home so do the best you can for us try to find Ros Mahan offise in Eclice Street N₂ 7 Dublin so do the best you can to bring us up to Dublin if you can your Mother Does not like to stop in Roscommon she would rather die in Doorty than...

From the townland of Dooherty, Patrick Hunt broke rank by giving information about the murder of Mahon. However, not all of his family members were given protection from the constabulary as this letter indicated.

with eviction. On Sunday, 1 November 1847, as he said mass in front of a packed congregation, McDermott allegedly criticized the clearances undertaken by Major Denis Mahon and ended by saying that 'he is worse than Cromwell and yet he lives'. For the secret societies who had been plotting and waiting their chance, this was seen as being the death knell for Strokestown's landlord.

Led by Andrew Connor, a notorious agrarian conspirator from Graffogue at the foot of the Sliabh Bawn mountain, the conspirators' initial plan was to murder Mahon towards the end of October. Connor did not act alone; if the police reports following the murder are to be believed, at least twenty people had prior knowledge of the affair.[9] On 2 November, shortly before 6 p.m., having attended a meeting of the Roscommon Board of Guardians where he had sought an extension of relief for the inhabitants of Strokestown, Mahon was ambushed and murdered. He was shot in the chest and died instantly. The news of his death quickly spread across Roscommon and was widely celebrated: 'bonfires were to be seen on the hills for many miles extent'.[10]

In the weeks and months that followed, police in Roscommon apprehended a number of suspects and although there was little evidence, many were lodged in gaol until a case could be brought against them.[11] However, the police met with several obstacles and even with credible evidence and testimony there were difficulties in making arrests. For example, after receiving information on a potential suspect, so common was the surname Cox on the Strokestown estate, that the police were at a loss as to who they should apprehend.[12] Although information was forthcoming, it was, to say the least, conflicting. Thomas Tiernan, for example, a pensioner in the 41st Regiment of Foot, claimed that while attending a shebeen in Elphin on the Saturday before the murder, he heard a man named Thomas Kelly lament the drowning of two boat loads of tenants (an untrue rumour) stating that 'it was a bad country that would allow such a person as the Major' to live.[13] Even Charles Costello, the relief committee clerk, was briefly implicated in the murder; Dr Shanley noted that 'in his youthful days he was accused of stealing small clothes, shoes and other low shably acts'.[14]

Officers followed suspects to England, where many had emigrated to Manchester, Derby and other towns, while a police constable was also sent to Montreal, Canada, to ascertain the whereabouts of Andrew Connor, who had evaded arrest. Indeed, as late as 1849 Thomas Brennan was apprehended in Peterborough, England. Despite the reward of over £800 offered by the Mahon family for the apprehension of the assassins, the police met with a wall of silence.[15] Martin Carrick, a constabulary officer, travelled through the townland of Dooherty but could get no assistance whatsoever from the local population.[16] Ross Mahon offered a stay of execution with eviction proceedings if anyone would turn informer. Conversely, some tenants were threatened with eviction unless information about the murder was forthcoming. Ross Mahon was confident that 'the threats made to the Cornashina tenants will have the desired effect'.[17]

There was another incentive for people to provide information. Those who were prepared to give evidence at the trial were to be rewarded with free passage to America and elsewhere. The idea of assisting witnesses in emigrating was first mooted by Major Denis Mahon's widow in early 1848 and in total thirty-one people provided evidence for the Crown. Henry Sandford Pakenham Mahon, the new owner of Strokestown, was kept up to date with the information that the people provided:

> We had a man under examination yesterday evening who swore that he was asked by Hasty to commit the murder and that he gave him pistols and told him he would be well paid. He is an old pensioner named Rigney and he was in custody before.[18]

Relief committees

In early 1846 the British government under Sir Robert Peel looked to Irish landowners to help shoulder the responsibility for relief. Across Ireland, 650 local relief committees were established with a central body, located in Dublin, coordinating their efforts. These committees raised local subscriptions, which were matched by government, thereby enabling the purchase of relief for those most in need. The local committees also oversaw the public work schemes. However, petty squabbling in parishes and baronies about who was responsible for various areas greatly hindered relief at a local level. This squabbling was essentially about boundaries and administration, on which agreement could not be reached. At Strokestown, for example, there was particular resentment towards Major Denis Mahon's choice of overseers on the public work schemes and his feud with Revd Michael McDermott may have had its origins in this matter. This failure to organize properly in order to engage with the crisis led to fundamental difficulties that might have been avoided had landlords, agents and others worked together for the benefit of the poor.

The families of those who were accused of involvement in the murder were struck from the relief lists in Strokestown, thereby exacerbating their plight. The mother of Michael Gardiner pleaded with her son to confess his involvement so that his family would be spared.

Ostracized by the local community for having provided evidence, some, like Patrick Hunt and Michael Donnelly, travelled to New Orleans with their families.[19] Little sympathy was given to the families of those implicated in the murder. Michael Gardiner's mother complained that she had been struck off the relief lists because of his involvement. Pleading with her imprisoned son, she implored him to tell the truth so as to spare his struggling family on the outside.[20] Three men were finally prosecuted and sentenced to be hanged for the crime: Patrick Hasty, James Cummins and Patrick Doyle. However, by the summer of 1848 interest had petered out in the Mahon murder trial and attention instead shifted to the Young Irelander trials in Dublin.[21]

The Mahon murder, and the controversies surrounding it, became an international news sensation. Several newspapers, including the *Freeman's Journal* and the *Nation*, laid blame for the murder squarely on the clearance of tenants and labelled Mahon as an 'ejector' of the poor. Indeed, the charge was reiterated by the British press; the *Morning Chronicle*, for example, condemned Mahon's policy of 'slow murder' – that is, the eviction of tenants.[22] International journals such as the *Bathurst Advocate* (New Zealand) carried news of the murder, claiming that lists were being posted on the road to Strokestown indicating who was to be murdered next.[23] In Australia the *Sydney Chronicle* gave wide coverage to the story as did the *Sydney Morning Herald*.[24] In the Vatican, Pope Pius IX was said to have been shocked by the murder and wished that the controversy would cease at once.[25] Queen Victoria personally lamented the murder, noting in her diary:

> A shocking murder has again taken place in Ireland. Major Mahon, who had entirely devoted himself to being of use to the distressed Irish, was shot when driving home in his carriage. Really they are a terrible people ... It is a constant source of anxiety and annoyance.[26]

Likewise, Prince Albert was said to have followed the murder trial and controversy with interest: 'the state of Ireland is fearful at the moment, there does not pass a day that some atrocious murder does not take place'.[27] Albert's interest in the case probably stemmed from his private secretary, Colonel Phipps, who was related to Major Mahon.[28] Others were also said to be outraged. Sir Randolph Routh, chairman of the relief commission, wrote of Major Mahon that 'a milder and more charitable man could not be found'.[29]

Appalled by what had happened, the editor of the *Cork Examiner* offered the following opinion:

> One day we record the havoc of the landlords of West Carbery, the next we are called upon to record the havoc of the peasants of Roscommon! Where is all this to end?[30]

In the House of Lords, the county Cavan landowner, Lord Farnham, attacked the Revd McDermott as 'the musket of the assassin was discharged at the man whom the priest had denounced the previous sabbath'.[31] He was ably supported by Lord Stanley who quipped that 'the man [Mahon] would be immortal if he survived that denunciation'.[32] Countering these claims Henry Grattan weighed in with a somewhat different perspective: 'Major Mahon said he would make a sheep walk of Strokestown. Within a fortnight afterwards he was shot.'[33] For his efforts, Grattan was rewarded with the charge that he was merely an 'apologist for the thugs of Roscommon'.[34]

> We further unhesitatingly declare that we never heard the Very Rev. Michael M‘Dermott, on Sunday or holiday, or Saints' Day, or any other day, on which he ever addressed his flock from the altar, to denounce the late Major Mahon, or to express the words attributed to him in the reported speech of Lord Farnham, or any SUCH words, or any words of a SIMILAR IMPORT or MEANING.
>
> LUKE CARLOS, Grocer, &c.
> NICHOLAS FAHY, Dealer.
> FRANCIS KENNY, Rope Dealer and Manufacturer.
> THOMAS CASSERLY, Slater and Plumber.
> JAMES DALY, Grocer.
> JOHN SMYTH, Farmer.
> PATRICK M‘GREENY, Farmer.
> JAMES CRUISE, Private Gentleman.
> J. F. CALLAGHAN, Woollen Draper, &c.
> DANIEL HUGHES, Farmer.
> MICHAEL O'BEIRNE, Wine and Spirit Merchant.
> PATRICK DOLAN, Woollen Draper, &c.
> PATRICK M‘MANUS,   ditto.
> JOHN LYNAM, Grocer, Wine, and Spirit Merchant.
> HUBERT CROGHAN,   ditto.
> PETER HEARY,   ditto.
> JOHN M‘MANUS, Grocer and Draper.
> JOHN HIGGINS, Publican.
> JAMES BRADY, Baker.
> JOHN GEARTY, Grocer, Wine, and Spirit Merchant.
> MICHAEL KELLY, Innkeeper.
> THOMAS DOLAN, Cartwright.
> WILLIAM CANNING, Victualler.
> JAMES O'BEIRNE. Chandler and ditto,
> EDWARD CONRY, Grocer, &c.
> BERNARD HAYDON, Whitesmith.
> OWEN MANNING, Grocer, &c.
> BERNARD GILL.
>   Strokestown, December 31st, 1847.

Although the local population had once offered deference to the Mahon family, in the dispute that followed the murder, the shopkeepers, merchants and tradesmen staunchly backed Revd Michael McDermott against the charge that he had cursed Mahon as being 'Worse than Cromwell'.

However, among the local population in Strokestown, and by extension county Roscommon, the reaction was quite different. According to one contemporary 'the people in the neighbourhood think the deed a holy one instead of a diabolical one'.[35]

The murder was also utilized by various political factions, ably aided by members of the press. The events in Strokestown were used to cast the Famine as a religious conflict.[36] As Donal Kerr has argued, the Mahon controversy showed the Catholic priesthood's 'growing alienation' from the British government.[37] It was somewhat ironic then that some of the priests and their supporters who were embroiled in the controversy profited from the clearances on the estate, as discussed below.

As the murder was debated in the House of Commons, John Ross Mahon compiled a 'memorandum of his management of the estate' in which he justified his actions since commencing the agency a year previously.

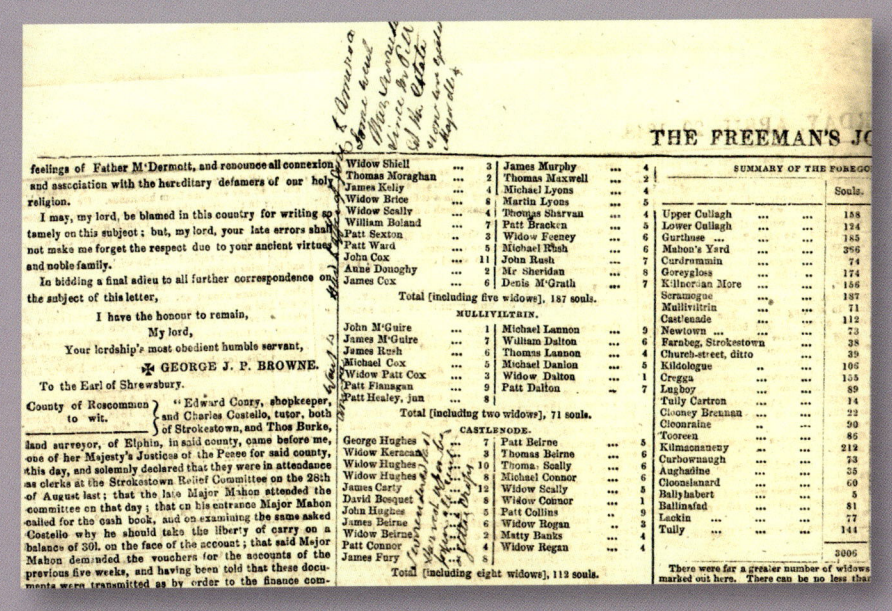

Embroiled in the controversy surrounding the Revd McDermott's alleged denunciation of Major Mahon, in April 1848 Bishop George Browne of Elphin published a list of tenants evicted from the Mahon estate. According to Browne, the evictions on the estate since Major Mahon had taken over amounted to 3,006 people. This copy of the *Freeman's Journal*, 29 April 1848, annotated by the Mahon family, highlights discrepancies where the family disputes the numbers evicted.

THE MURDER OF MAJOR MAHON   103

The new owner of the estate, Henry Sandford Pakenham Mahon, was determined to restore order and began by advertising for the letting of farms on the estate in March 1848.

Responding to the crisis, Bishop Browne of Elphin quickly defended his parish priest against any wrongdoing and described McDermott as an 'innocent and much maligned priest'.[38] What followed was a serious of tit-for-tat allegations. In an effort to discredit the evidence of the bishop, Ross Mahon highlighted the fact that Browne's brother, Patrick, was a middleman on the estate and had evicted under-tenants on his holding at Cloonfad. He alleged: 'the bishop's brother expressed a hope of being able to liquidate the arrears if given time' but took advantage of the situation and 'put out every tenant who had not paid up his rent'.[39] Denying that he knew anything of the conduct of his brother, the bishop in turn publicly listed over 3,000 people who had been evicted from the estate. Significantly, the list of evicted tenants published by Bishop Browne in the *Freeman's Journal* did not include any from his family's townland of Cloonfad.[40] Neither does the list make any distinction between eviction and the assisted emigration scheme. Publicly backing the bishop, the *Freeman's Journal* highlighted the plight of the Mahon tenantry and carried headlines such as: 'Extermination by the thousand' and the 'Tenant Right! – Extermination'. Anxious to counteract the bishop's claims, Ross Mahon responded by arguing that:

> As regards the list published by Bishop Browne of Elphin those persons who have been evicted, or who have surrendered their holdings on the Strokestown estate, and which seems to have been done as a means of palliating the murder of Major Mahon … I wish to mention that the greater portion of it is composed of persons whose buildings we got possession of once Major Mahon was murdered.[41]

The merchant and business classes of Strokestown also lent their voice to the debate to declare that the Revd McDermott did not denounce Mahon before he was shot and to offer support to their clergyman.[42] In his defence the Revd McDermott outlined that it was the clearance of tenants that had contributed to the murder of Major Denis Mahon:

> The infamous and inhuman cruelties which were wantonly and unnecessarily exercised against a tenantry, whose feelings were already wound up to woeful and vengeful exasperation by the loss of their exiled relatives, as well as by hunger and pestilence, which swept so many victims to an untimely grave – in my opinion may be assigned as the sole exciting cause of the disastrous event which occurred. I saw no necessity for the idle display of such a large force of military and police, carrying outside so many rounds of ball cartridge, and inside some substantial rounds of whiskey, bacon and bakers bread, surrounding the poor

> man's cabin, setting fire to the roof while the half starved, half naked children were hastening away from the flames with yells of despair, while the mother lay prostrate on the threshold of agony, and the heartbroken father remained supplicating on his knees ... in my opinion these scenes, of which I can only draw a very inefficient portrait, had more to do with the murder of Major Mahon than all the thundering denunciations the Vatican could effect, had they been rolled on his head.[43]

In the months following the murder of his father-in-law, Henry Sandford Pakenham Mahon was advised to leave the Strokestown estate to its own devices for the foreseeable future. The county Galway landowner, Denis Kelly, suggested that:

> Society in Roscommon is completely disorganised and it will take years to reconstruct the social fabric there, particularly under the 'laissez faire' system of the Whigs, and under such circumstances my advice to you is to forget for five years at least that you have such a thing as property in Roscommon, to leave it totally in the hands of your agent. Amuse yourself and your dear wife as youth and circumstance will, for the present, and trust to a gracious Providence that at that time you will have a chance of returning to an altered country and breaking entirely fresh ground. I think Galway will recover much sooner and that if peace can be preserved another year will see us much as usual here, but in Roscommon [particularly your part of it] I have no hopes of any real improvement for five years.[44]

Pakenham Mahon was keen to continue the clearances in order to facilitate the introduction of a new tenantry, and also to punish those who were guilty by association of the murder. Ross Mahon backed these plans and hoped that Pakenham Mahon's 'offer' to certain tenants would have the 'desired effect' in bringing forth information.

The secret societies soon turned their attention to Pakenham Mahon, informing him that he would soon suffer the same fate as his kinsman, 'the Demon Major Mahon'.

THE MURDER OF MAJOR MAHON

List of persons in the following Townlands from whom possession was taken by the Sheriff of the County Roscommon on the 20. 21. 23 & 25th September 1848. and handed over to me on the part of the Proprietor Henry Sandford Packenham Mahon Esq.

	Houses Levelled	Offices Levelled	Observations
On the 20th— Dooerty—			
1 Patrick Hunt	House		
2 Bryan Flynn	House		
3 Thady Hunt	House & barn		
4 Edmond Dwyer	House		
5 James Donnelly	House — & Offices		
	Walls		unoccupied
6 John Bay	House & Offices		
— Hunt - Widow — 21st	House		
7 James Carroll	House		
8 James Farrell	House & Offices		
9 Martin Tighe	House & Offices		
10 Michl. Donnelly	House		levelled by himself
11 Elias Salt	House		
12 Cathne Hunt Widow	House		
13 Thady Hunt	House		
14 Pat Hunt	House		
15 Mary Tremble	House		
16 Pat Kelly	House		
17 Michl. Gardner	Walls of out house		
18 Do			Signed an acknowledgement by his wife
19 John Macnamara			Signed an acknowledgement

The townlands of Dooherty, Cornashina and Castle Leitrim, among others, were once again targeted in a new wave of clearances during 1848–9, as this document shows.

A continued depression in agricultural matters was also said have greatly affected farming concerns and once prosp tenants were now reduced to 'a state of starvation'.

7

'With Renewed Vigour': the Clearances Continued

> The rueful effects of extermination which is even now going on with unceasing severity, may be witnessed from one extremity to the other of this ill-fated parish. I am fully convinced that no part of Ireland — not excepting Schull or Skibbereen — has suffered more from Famine, extermination, and various infectious diseases, which have reduced the population of my parish ... from about nine thousand six hundred souls to three thousand.[1]

In 1848 an already impoverished Strokestown was devastated by the appearance of fever, particularly cholera and typhus. At this time houses were being levelled on an almost-daily basis.[2] A violent storm in December decimated the makeshift accommodation of many paupers, primarily on the edges of bog.[3] In addition, a continued depression in agriculture was said to have greatly affected farming concerns and once-prosperous tenants were now reduced to 'a state of starvation'.[4]

As the new owner of the Strokestown estate, Henry Sandford Pakenham Mahon did not waste any time in asserting his authority. He applied his new rigorous estate management policy to the contentious townland of Dooherty as an example to those who might conspire to murder or withhold rent in the future: 'The more I think of the Dooherty tenants the more necessary it appears to me that a strong example should be made of the whole townland' he wrote in January 1848.[5] The message to others was also quite clear: 'If there are any who can pay up the rent they owe either to the executors of Major Mahon or to the middlemen we will retain them upon them doing so'.[6] For those who could not, no extra allowance was to be made to assist with emigration or for surrendering their holdings.[7]

Somewhat surprisingly, 'no defences were made' against this new round of evictions, despite Ross Mahon's belief that tenants would stick to their holdings with 'greater pertinacity than ever'.[8] Over 40 policemen oversaw the affair, evidence perhaps of expected trouble.[9] Given more than eight months to remove, the bailiffs finally began the levelling of dwellings in September 1848 when over 105 families were evicted from five townlands. In total, this eviction involved more than 1,000 people. All houses were levelled, and in some cases the task was performed by the people themselves.[10] These clearances were retribution for the murder of Major Mahon, as can be seen in Ross Mahon's admission that tenants at Cornashina were 'possibly worth some consideration though it is scarcely probable that they were not in some measure privy to what was going on'.[11] The same was true at Clonscara where tenants were

Throughout 1848 and 1849, eviction and clearance on the Strokestown estate was so widespread that little opposition was offered by the local population.

The distraining of crops and animals in lieu of rent was a tactic favoured by agents and bailiffs alike. The distrained goods were then brought to the local market where they were sold.

described as 'peculiarly bad and owed a great deal of rent'.[12] In the eyes of the public, revenge was finally enacted for the murder. However, not all were comfortable with this turn of events and even Ross Mahon himself had reservations and offered advice to his employer about how best to proceed with clearances. In particular, he stressed the need to give gratuities to those who were cleared, in an effort to avoid 'great annoyance'.[13] The advice went unheeded.[14] It was now believed that it was better to create breathing space for the more industrious tenants, and those who were unwilling to adopt new agricultural practices were not to be helped.[15] The latter were described as 'useless' tenants.[16] Also singled out were those who had contracted disease and some, like Roger Murray, whose family were 'continually relapsing in fever', were denied compensation for 'levelling his house to the foundation'.[17]

The decimation caused by clearances and the levelling of houses was only too apparent to visitors to county Roscommon in 1848; for example, Thomas Wynne Boggs noted that:

> With the assistance of the clergy, I have been endeavouring to ascertain the quantity of tillage land in this splendid county of Roscommon, and we think it is about five acres tilled for forty-five acres untilled and lying idle. The great part of these rich and beautiful plains is covered with weeds and rushes. The people are wandering about, seeking for foreign food for breaking stones; their families starving; and that beautiful land, that ought to support them all and as many more, is lying idle like themselves and useless.[18]

Pakenham Mahon was not the only landlord who engaged in this clearance policy, which had been made all the more effective by the introduction of the so-called Gregory or 'Quarter Acre' clause in 1848, which stipulated that holders of more than a quarter of an acre of land could not be deemed destitute and entitled to relief.[19]

The clearances were so numerous that they often went unreported, and scenes such as depicted here would have been commonplace throughout the country.

STR/109.

To John Robinson

take Notice that Michal Kinney of Farmley and Thomas Covahey is Collecting Mony to Shoot you as Kinney is the Appronted Collitor in this Nighbourhood and also he was the Collitor of the Mony for the Shooting of Major Mahon for it is in his house the fowler Slept and was in Kings house waiting for King to Collect the Mony to Robinson I am a frind and has a great wish for you and I would Mintion My Name but if it was knowen I would be Shot

As eviction and clearance continued on the Pakenham Mahon estate, bailiffs, hut tumblers and 'watchers' were frequently threatened and beaten. This threatening letter informed the bailiff, John Robinson, that money was being collected to have him shot.

> PP/STR/64(17)
>
> Castlenode 3 mo 19th 1853
>
> Dear T Roberts
>
> Of the 5 houses on Cloneen I would prefer putting the people out of 2 only — the Widow Gardiner whose house I wish to keep up to put my horses in when I go there myself or when I have horses working on the farm until I build — & Pat Sweeny's wife who has the 2 acres of bog & whose house I want for the herd or for one of the other 3 men, should the herd prefer another of the houses instead of hers — The best house is that at the right hand side of the road & now occupied by Gardiner above mentioned intended for horses & the other end of it by Wade who I think may remain in it unless the herd prefers it to Sweeny's — Wade who with 3 sons full grown — Patt McGarry with 2 sons & 1 daughter full grown, & [...]

The callousness of some people during the Famine is exemplified in this letter of 1853 where George Walpole indicates that he wanted to evict the widow Gardiner from lands at Cloneen as he wished to keep horses in her house.

MAP of CASTLENODE FARM
IN PARTS OF THE
TOWNLANDS of NEWTOWN, BUMLIN, & CASTLENODE
PARISH of BUMLIN
BARONY AND COUNTY of
ROSCOMMON
The Property of M. S. Pakenham Mahon Esq.

Roscommon landlords such as Peter Keogh and Charles O'Connor were strongly criticized for carrying out evictions on their estates.[20] However, it was the actions of Strokestown estate officials that resulted in the area becoming a byword for mass-eviction. Indeed, an indication of their zealousness was revealed in their proposal to auction on Christmas Day crops and animals seized for non-payment of rent.[21] On other occasions, evictions had been carried out in appalling conditions, such as at Lisbrid and Newtown in April 1850, where tenants were evicted in terrible 'storm and rain'.[22] This period also saw the social rise of lower level estate officials, including bailiffs and watchers, who would make decisions as to who was to be cleared and who should remain. In 1849, for example, when assessing tenants at Knockbarnaboy, Thomas Roberts, the under-agent, coldly concluded that 'there are twenty families on the land. Twelve of who are considered to be paupers and the remaining eight would be able to hold the rest of the land should they be let'.[23] But the motivation for the removal of other tenants was often personal. George Walpole was open about the reasons for removing tenants at Cloneen:

> Of the 5 houses in Cloneen I would prefer putting the people out of 2 only, the widow Gardiner whose house I wish to keep up to put my horses in when I go there myself or when I have horses working on the farm until I build, and Pat Sweeneys wife who has the 2 acres of bog.[24]

Although reluctant at first to continue the clearances, largely because of his concerns for his own safety, Ross Mahon soon changed his mind and was pleased with the progress of the hut tumblers, cheerfully informing his employer that:

> I am happy to say that the haberes have been executed without any incident or disturbance. The levelling of the houses has been done most effectively — there is not a wall left standing and the stones are removed to the foundation.[25]

The decision was now taken to target the remaining middlemen, as it avoided the public censure that eviction would bring, and also because many were now said to be 'in bad circumstances'.[26] Those targeted with 'renewed vigour' included George Knox, the former agent of the Ballykilcline estate, who was in financial difficulty. Although he had spent over £1,100 on improvements in the past, by May 1849 Knox could not find £63 to pay the rent.[27] Having sought lenience to be allowed sell his crops and animals at the Strokestown fair, Knox lambasted Pakenham Mahon, reminding him that 'every landlord in Ireland is giving an abatement and indulgence to their tenants these times and one month's extension of time'.[28] Others, like Robert Devenish, who were influential middlemen prior to the Famine, were now to be done away with.[29] The targeted middlemen also included the bishop of Elphin's brother, Patrick Browne, the former agent of the estate, Thomas Conry, and the Church of Ireland rector, Revd Joseph Morton. In December 1848 bailiffs moved to distrain Morton's lands at Castlecoote where arrears amounted to £205. The inventory of the stock seized by the bailiff highlighted the amount of capital available during the Famine and yet people were reluctant to pay rent, largely because those around them had refrained from doing so. The stock included:

> one bull, five cows, a two-year-old heifer, eight yearling heifers, two bullocks, two calves, three horses, three cocks of hay, two stacks of wheat, two stacks of oats, three carts, one plough and two reins.[30]

The ending of the public work schemes in late 1847 and the introduction of the 'Gregory' clause swelled the numbers of people who clamoured to be admitted to the workhouse.

Name			
Dominick Dennigan	2	14	S on Struck off
Eliza Brennan	3	21	S on Struck off
Mary Connor	6	29	off Beggar + Began living at the Bridge of Cootlanade
Mary Goblin	1	7	S on Struck off
Maggy Doolan	2	14	Struck off put on again
Cathn Lannon	4	21	Struck off
Michael Connor	3	17½	Con.
Thos. Fury	6	28	S off
Jane Kelly	1	7	Struck off
Margt. King	4	17½	Children Query relief
Ellen Carty	"	"	Struck off. Put on from the 1st November
James Carty	0	20¾	Struck off
Ellen Farrell	2	14	S off
Thos. Elwood	2	14	Struck off

As the Famine progressed, more attention was paid to those claiming relief. Where people were found to be 'impersonating' or not entitled to relief they were simply 'struck off'.

THE CLEARANCES CONTINUED

Landlords were safe in the knowledge that tenants would be found to take up land, as was the case with Lisbride House as seen from the letter above.

This was not an isolated case and, as will be discussed below, it provokes questions about culpability during the Great Famine and whether certain sections of the community could have done more to relieve local poverty.[31] The targeting of the middleman also meant the removal of his under-tenants and this drew widespread criticism: the *Roscommon Journal* commented that the 'crusade against the tenantry is daily increasing'.[32] Likewise, in January 1849, when over 250 ejectments went undefended at the Strokestown petty sessions, the *Freeman's Journal* commented that:

Although a team of 'watchers' were employed across the estate, tenants informed the agent of the number of cattle, sheep and other animals in the possession of other tenants in order to win the agent's favour.

> Depopulation is so general that it does not excite surprise or astonishment to hear of hundreds being daily turned to the ditches to famish ... tenant and small farmer gone to a happier country ... the poorer classes have either perished or are in the workhouse ... thousands of acres have not a beast upon them.[33]

Amid this lingering desolation tenants took the opportunity to inform on their neighbours, particularly if it helped stay an eviction notice.[34] Trespassing, access to turbary and the illegal grazing of cattle on land were among the major complaints brought to agents' attention.[35] The situation deteriorated to the point where it was claimed that 'the tenants are at war every day'. By 1852 many were said to 'have had enough of blood'.[36] A team of 'watchers' was employed throughout the estate to inform on the movement of crops and animals, and on the accumulation of money. They were also there to watch 'outgoing' or emigrating tenants, who, while preparing to go to America and elsewhere, 'generally permit every sort of trespass to be committed on the premises'. There were those like John Bruen, a strong farmer, who carefully watched land that was now lying idle in the hope that the agent 'may

THE CLEARANCES CONTINUED   121

Evictions and clearances

In the early stages of the Famine, landlords and their agents granted abatements of rent, forgave arrears or allowed reduced payment. However, by early 1847, with their resources now stretched, it was apparent to many landowners that abatements could not continue. Forced to pay the poor law rate for those whose holdings were valued at under £4, it was this class that many landlords targeted. In addition, middlemen were removed largely because they had been granted long and favourable leases during times of economic prosperity, which landlords now wanted to break, but also because their removal meant that their sub-tenants would be evicted. In order to avoid censure many landlords drafted estate rules, which, when broken, provided the pretext for eviction. The policy of clearances was further bolstered by the Gregory or 'Quarter Acre' clause introduced in 1848. While official records of the numbers evicted only began in 1849, it has been estimated that as many as 250,000 families were evicted from their homes during the Famine. More were evicted in the early 1850s as landlords wished to make their estates more attractive for would-be purchasers in the Encumbered Estates Court.

think of recommending it to myself'.[37] Simmering discontent also existed over the swapping of tenancies and the relocation of tenants. In a number of cases tenants were deemed unsuitable to farm certain holdings and so were swapped with more progressive farmers. Incoming tenants were often harassed, beaten and, in general, ostracized. The clearances also came at a cost to the estate, as tenants removed everything of value including the window panes and door frames of houses.[38] Renewed religious conflict also added significantly to tensions. Coming to a head in 1852, when the hotly contested election threatened the peace and stability of the country, animosity verged on paranoia:

> The priests are at their usual trade of denouncing and more particularly their fury is quite directed to the House of Strokestown. This ought to be a blessing to all Landlords not to encourage Popish tenants, get rid of them and you'll get rid of the priests.[39]

Ross Mahon granted compensation to over 140 tenants upon surrendering their holdings, hoping that this goodwill gesture would negate the growing unrest.[40] His hopes were misplaced. The evicted and starving took the law into their own hands and again resorted to violence, to the point where it was claimed that the people rejoiced when an outrage was committed.[41] The threat of violence was not lost on Ross Mahon who, as late as 1851, required a patrol of police to escort him to and from Strokestown.[42] Unsurprisingly, the hut tumblers and levellers were the focus

Not all of those who were cleared from the estate emigrated and some were left to build makeshift accommodation on the edges of bog, depending entirely on begging for their survival.

THE CLEARANCES CONTINUED   *123*

> I propose and promise to pay Henry
> S. P. Mahon Esqr. or his Heirs the sum
> of Two pounds sterl. yearly rent out
> of the small house which I occupy in
> the south side Elphin street Strokestown
> with a small plot that is to the rere of
> the said house (about a half an acre) rent
> to be commenced 1st November 1849
>
> To John R. Mahon Esqr.   John Costello
> Strokestown House

> I &c propose and will undertake to pay to
> Henry Sandford Pakingham Mahon Esqr or his
> Receivers Any Rent Yearly & Every Year that your
> Honour May think proper to lay on Eight Acres
> of land Situate in Tulsky & ofspring Minors Tulsks
> Property And formerly in the possion of Thomas Byrne
> Now in Your Honours possesion & joins the land that I hold
> Any Security Required for the payments of Rent Can
> be Produced   Patt Feehely of
> Dated Feby 11th 1851   Ballyfum

Tenants like John Costello and Pat Feehely undertook a promise in writing to pay an annual rent to the estate for their holdings. Such agreements suited landlords as it meant that the tenant had no recourse to the law, and could be evicted with ease.

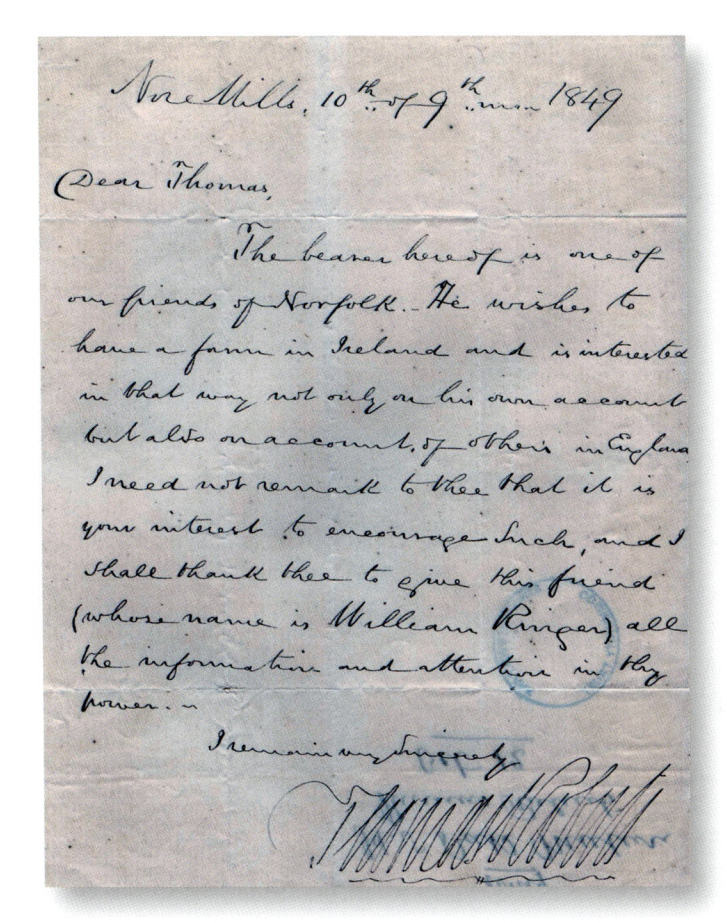

Hoping to introduce more progressive farmers and ultimately increase the rental, Ross Mahon targeted farmers from Scotland and Norfolk. However, largely owing to the rural unrest, these hoped-for tenants never arrived in large numbers.

of much of the violence. After one clearance, John Robinson, the bailiff, was rather bluntly informed: 'take notice that Michael Kinney of Farnbeg and Thomas Conahy is collecting money to shoot you'.[43] Another bailiff had his fingers broken when he seized crops for non-payment of rent and was advised by the doctor 'that one of the joints must be cut off'.[44] The detested middlemen also received similar threatening letters stating that the Molly Maguires would have their vengeance for the removing of under-tenants. George Walpole was warned:

> You need not think that the country is so beat yet as that they will listen to you ... you may keep the house for I am the man who will watch you day and night if you don't change your mind.[45]

THE CLEARANCES CONTINUED   125

PP/STR/29(55)

Fenloe
Newmarket on Fergus
County Clare
July 17th 1851

Sir,
              Gentleman
A Highly respectable, in my immediate neighbourhood has been enquiring of me respec=ting some farms appearing in the papers for sale in the County Roscommon, not being thoroughly acquaint with the locality in which they were situated I could give no information about them, but as he has an anxiety to become a resident in that County, if a suitable place would offer, the extent of which from 60 to 80 acres of good land, and as you, when I was in the Roscommon district, as practical Instructor under Lord Clarendon had a good many such places for sale on the Strokestown property. I recommended him to write you on the subject which

The land agent then turned his attention to attracting Irish farmers, like William Lindsay of Newmarket on Fergus, county Clare, to take up land on the estate.

> To The Honourable Lady of
> Henry S. Pakenham Mahon Esqr &c.
>
> The Humble petition of Pat
> Dogherty of Strokestown
>
> Most respectfully States
>
> That your ladyships
> Petitioner begs leave to inform you that
> your most Benevolent Father in his
> Lifetime Esteemed petitioner to far
> A greater Extent than the other inhabit
> =ants of Strokestown So far as follow
> About one month before the death of
> your much Regretted father the petete
> Proposed quiting his holding of the lai
> of Strokestown for which your father wa
> Sorry and told pet:r he would give h
> Bestow on him a years rent on which pe
> Did consent Still to occupy his hold

In the months that followed the murder of Major Denis Mahon, several tenants wrote to the land agent informing him that they had got a personal guarantee from the landlord that they would be allowed to remain in their holding.

THE CLEARANCES CONTINUED

Understandably, the Famine brought with it a decline in social morals and gave rise to anti-social behaviour. For example, the appearance of a brothel in an abandoned house on the Strokestown estate was a cause of scandal in the early 1850s. Estate officials were outraged to learn that the house was a venue where 'all the improper women of the town spend the nights in the house with their evil companions'.[46] As a result, the agent's duties now included enforcing a strict code of ethics on the Strokestown estate, explaining to those who protested that immorality had been a determining factor in their poverty. Ross Mahon now attempted to remove other trouble makers and those involved in crime. These included Daniel Mullooly and his wife who 'turned out to be notorious robbers' and Terry McKeon who 'turned out to be a scandle [sic] to the townland' as 'no persons character is safe from him or his villianous tonge, male or female'.[47] Others were dismissed for their involvement in threatening and intimidating behaviour.[48]

With no end of famine in sight, the people of Strokestown sought assistance and lenience from their landlord. The Strokestown archive provides examples of tenants, often in harrowing circumstances, daily petitioning for help. Although the petitions are similar in tone, many seem to have been penned by the individuals themselves, suggesting a level of literacy among the Mahon tenantry. The petitions provide an insight and a voice to those most affected by the Famine. For example, Thomas O'Farrell of Ballinafad lamented that he was now struggling since 'the recent shock which has deranged our social interests'.[49] The petition of the widow Cox of Scramogue begged for a 'morsel of food' for her grandchildren, who had been abandoned by their father.[50] The desperation of some, like Pat Wallace of Culliagh, could be seen in his desire to be allowed a small portion of waste cutaway bog where he could take his large family. He was, in his own words, 'out of my senses seeing ruin and destruction on my family'.[51] The petitions also confirm the contemporary belief that it was divine providence that had caused the blight, or as the Widow Burke suggested 'god in his infinite mercies afflicted the people with the loss of their potatoes'.[52] Social isolation, where family had died, emigrated or in some cases simply abandoned one another, is also revealed in the petitions.[53] For example, a tenant named Maguire, described as being 'deaf, dumb and orphaned and destitute of friends', begged for relief as he had no one else to support him.[54]

Hunger was not the only threat to these tenants; they also often struggled with the lack of shelter. The widow Catherside feared that her children would become 'urchins to the cold' if not provided with shelter.[55] Others feared for the safety and health of their children if faced with eviction.[56] Penned by Patrick Kilmartin, perhaps one of the more unusual petitions came in the form of a poem, part of which read:

1P/STR/20(22)

Rockville 20 May 1850

Sir

The Bearer John Cox of Corricklim under Tenant to Bryan Redican, solicits me to recommend him to you, as a Tenant capable of holding seven acres of Land.

I have known him upwards of twenty years, during which period he has been in my employment as day labourer (one of the very few who required no eye after him) he is honest, sober, quiet and most industrious, being in possession of two fine milch Cows. and two yearling Heiffers, all

Many tenants obtained letters of recommendation which assured that they were trustworthy and could be relied upon to pay their rent.

THE CLEARANCES CONTINUED

Bailiffs were encouraged to undertake extensive surveys of the estate in order to estimate what portion lay waste, to ascertain the circumstances of individual tenants and in some cases to see who had survived. This survey of conacre in Ballinafad in June 1848 by William Mara was a case in point.

> In the year of 50 I lost my wife, by a cruel fever in that strife, in that infection my children lay, which delay my payment to this day.[57]

Collective petitions also outlined the extent of the problems at Strokestown. In August 1848 the Ballinafad tenants implored the Revd Pakenham, Dean of St Patrick's Cathedral in Dublin, to use his influence and persuade his son to help them. Part of their appeal read:

> I take the opportunity of addressing you a second time stating the condition of the former tenants of Ballinafad who is cast upon the misfortune of the world doomed to seek food and shelter and cannot find it, to add to our misfortune we starved ourselves in order to make a crop of potatoes in hopes to have some food for the winter coming but our hopes is blasted in consequence of the failure of the crop and no chance of living remains for us. We have neither money or value.[58]

In the majority of cases it is not known whether these requests were granted. By 1851 clearance and eviction in Roscommon was so widespread it was feared that the whole county would soon become a 'wilderness'.[59] Those who were spared the depredations of the previous decade and the wrath of the landlord now faced an uncertain future. These survivors included the tenants at Culleen who were said to be outraged when it was suggested that there existed a conspiracy to murder among them.[60] Regardless of their claims, the Culleen tenants and others were now issued with an ultimatum: those who could not pay up rent and arrears due at the end of 1851 were to be ejected, as they were deemed to be 'backward tenants'.[61] For the evicted, the newly opened workhouse in Strokestown was now their only place of sanctuary, albeit their last option. Conditions there were appalling and 'inmates' were given a diet of damaged Indian corn. Refusing to enter the workhouse, many relied on outdoor relief and whatever assistance was given locally. Many erected temporary huts and makeshift accommodation. Over time they were removed permanently from the estate.[62]

By the mid-1850s there was evidence of a softening approach to estate management. Tenants like Mick O'Beirne, who made several attempts to pay his rent, were retained as they had displayed signs of improving their holdings.[63] Likewise, writing in November 1855, in relation to ejectments, Pakenham Mahon noted:

> Though I should be glad to get rid of the cabins on Church St or the new Fair Green, as quickly as possible — I should not wish those who are building elsewhere to be thrust out of their present abodes before they have their news ones tolerably comfortable.[64]

Despite his previous actions, even Ross Mahon appears to have acted with some compassion. In 1855, for example, he ordered that although it was time to remove cabins on Elphin Street 'I did not like disturbing the inhabitants during the winter – you may give gratuities from £1 to £1 10s. on their leaving and forgive arrears of rent'.[65] However, by the decade's end arrears had once again accumulated and the estate was poised for a new wave of evictions. In 1859 Ross Mahon informed tenants that 'they had better be warned to attend to pass their notes'.[66] The agent was adamant that he would 'not fall without a struggle'.[67]

Edwin O'Beirne, a Strokestown Famine emigrant, was killed in Missouri during the American Civil War, 1863.

In August 1852 potato blight at Strokestown was said to be making its appearance so extensively – it is very alarming. At the monthly meeting of the town's Board of Guardians the Union's agriculturalist gave a display of diseased pot

8

The Exodus Continues

> In Roscommon, so extensive is the emigration, that for miles the land is wilderness, and it is a race with the peasants and the farmers who shall first reach the emigrant ship.[1]

The reappearance of the potato blight in the early 1850s dramatically swelled the numbers emigrating from Ireland. Areas of the Midlands such as King's County, Longford, Westmeath and Roscommon were severely affected by the continued presence of *Phytophthora infestans*. In August 1852 potato blight at Strokestown was said to be 'making its appearance so extensively – it is very alarming'.[2] At the monthly meeting of the town's Board of Guardians, the Union's agriculturalist put on a display of diseased potatoes, indicating, perhaps, that the problems associated with blight were still misunderstood.[3] The following summer the potato crop once again failed and Thomas Roberts, the under-agent, was informed that 'the potatoes are blighted & if the disease should continue to become worse I think you should make a vast reduction in the rents of your tenants'.[4] Amid much panic there was renewed outrage and violence, the most serious incident being the murder of Andrew Herans in September 1852. Described as a 'confidential man', or agent, to Alonzo Lauder, Herans was attacked and beaten by three men and later died from his injuries.[5] The murder was only one of a number of crimes that were committed in Roscommon as lawlessness prevailed.[6]

A substantial number – possibly in the region of 3,000 people – from the Strokestown estate emigrated during the years 1848–54. Indeed, such was the level of emigration that the Strokestown Board of Guardians feared that there would be insufficient

Matilda O'Beirne (1840–1928), who emigrated to Missouri during the Famine.

numbers to till the land if the exodus continued.[7] The desperation of people was once again evident in the number of petitions that were sent to Pakenham Mahon seeking assistance in emigrating. Although these petitions were largely on an individual or family basis, there were some exceptions, as the case of the Kilbeg tenants illustrates:

> Sir, we the remaining tenants of Kilbeg are anxious to know whether you will emigrate us to America or encourage us to make a crop. And if we are to remain in Kilbeg we will make a good crop and pay a year's rent when the harvest comes in.[8]

As the Famine wore on, the emigrants included the sons and daughters of once-prosperous farmers such as John Rush, who in 1848 sought assistance in sending his children to America.

THE DEGRADED CELT.—In our last number we had occasion to allude to an example of enterprise, and of affectionate regard for his family, on the part of a liberated Irish convict, which has few examples—in our present, we have an almost similar pleasing account before us, and of a party from the same locality—Strokestown. Frank Coggins, with his son, wife, and three daughters were received for admission at the Strokestown workhouse in March, 1850—and a more wretched and emaciated looking set could scarce be found even within the walls of such an institution. After little more than a month's residence, Coggins with his son, a youth of fifteen, absconded, leaving wife and family in the house, probably according to a previous arrangement between them. The men went to England, earned a little there, what paid their passage to America, which they reached about nine months ago. On last week the master of the Strokestown workhouse received from the father and son in America the passage tickets for the family, whom they had to leave in the workhouse in Ireland.—*Roscommon Messenger*.

In March 1850, Frank Coggins, his wife and four children entered Strokestown workhouse where they were described as 'wretched and emaciated'. Absconding from the workhouse two weeks later with his 15-year-old son, Coggins made first for England, and then reached America in early 1852. Having earned enough money, he sent passage tickets to the master of the workhouse for his wife and three daughters. The extract from the Strokestown Board of Guardian minute books in September 1852 indicates that the guardians gave their consent to the family emigrating.

The anxieties of the Kilbeg tenants were apparent elsewhere. Fearing for his family's welfare Alex Ballintine looked for assistance in recovering 'fifty shillings for me which would be of great use to my helpless family going to a foreign land'.[9] It was the same desperation that drove the once-prosperous farmer, John Rush, to seek:

> some fair or reasonable compensation whatever you may think proper to enable me to send my son and daughter to America that they may provide for themselves what I am not able to support them.[10]

136 STROKESTOWN AND THE GREAT IRISH FAMINE

No record survives of whether Rush received assistance but others were fortunate; George Carton, for example, and his large family were given £10 to emigrate to New York.[11] Indeed, so anxious were people to emigrate that many resorted to crime in the hope that they would be transported, something that prompted Major Denis Mahon to conclude wryly that 'many of those fellows like to travel for the benefit of their health'.[12] Among those sentenced to transportation were Pat Dillon for stealing a donkey; Pat Flynn for stealing a heifer; John Timon and Pat McGuire who committed larceny, and Luke Farrell for sheep stealing.[13] Emigrating tenants were also buoyed by the fact that there was no shortage of people to buy their stock, indicating the level of wealth that still abounded.[14] Contrary to the behaviour of the stereotypical middleman, some acted with charity towards emigrating under-tenants, illustrated best by a Mr Kelly of Four Mile House, near Strokestown, who was reported to have brought fifty under-tenants with him to America. Prior to the Famine he was said to have more than £10,000 in savings.[15] However, not everyone was enamoured by the prospect of the new world. William Flood of Strokestown, for example, was of the opinion that 'a man can get on far better in Ireland than in America'.[16]

Although there had been lingering negative publicity surrounding the 1847 assisted emigration scheme, Guinness & Mahon continued to encourage emigrants to travel to Quebec and other Canadian ports.[17] This was largely because by 1852 the cost of passage to Quebec had halved, allowing more tenants the opportunity to go. In addition, there was also plentiful employment to be found in a number of Canadian cities:

> The passage to Quebec costs £3 15s. for an adult besides about £1 10s. for bedding. There is sure employment in Quebec ... for able bodied laborers on the extensive railways in progress there – servant girls are also sure of employment.[18]

Others chose different destinations and by the early 1850s Strokestown emigrants were to be found in Australia, South America, the US, Britain and South Africa.

Patrick Mally, for example, had settled in Van Diemen's Land (Tasmania) and endeavoured to secure the passage of family and friends to the island. Henry Sandford Pakenham Mahon paid for the passage of 'two Cowan girls on an assisted passage to the Canterbury settlement in New Zealand, a thriving colony, a splendid climate'.[19] As this case demonstrates, Pakenham Mahon was willing to finance the emigration of certain tenants. These included the Doherty family who were given passage to

As late as 1852, Guinness & Mahon, land agents, still wanted to send tenants from Strokestown to Quebec.

Patrick Hanly (1834–1920), who emigrated from Strokestown during the Famine, was a noted railroad worker in Maryland, US.

Baltimore and Mick O'Hara who was given £5 'to go to America' in 1852.[20] Naturally, Strokestown natives were to be found scattered across Britain, where pre-Famine links had been established through seasonal migration. These included, for example, the Lennons in Manchester, the Duffy brothers in Rawmarsh, Yorkshire, and the Noones in Derby. Others used Britain as a stepping stone before emigrating to America, as in the case of John Flynn who finally settled in Illinois in 1860. This process, known as chain migration, was the experience of many Famine emigrants.[21]

These later emigrants fared somewhat better than those who had travelled in 1847 and earlier. Largely because of the public condemnation following the 1847 scheme, emigrants were provided with further provisions for their journey. For example, in April 1855 Jane Neylor of Strokestown was among a number of tenants assisted in emigrating to Philadelphia.[22] Among the items she was provided with for the voyage were 1lb of tea, 1lb of coffee, 5lbs of sugar; bacon, red herring; one stone of biscuit, flour, a frying pan, a knife and fork, a pair of blankets and calico for making bed tick.[23] Many emigrants were determined to settle their accounts before they left; Denis Sweeney, for example, sought to clear his arrears before emigrating to Melbourne, Australia.[24]

Another notable feature of the Strokestown emigrants was the number of women, like Bridget Hanly, who chose to emigrate alone and with no apparent network of friends or family at their chosen destination. Some failed to adapt and were forced to resort to crime, as was the case with Mary Wilson in Edinburgh, Scotland.[25] The age profile of the Strokestown emigrants is also noteworthy. Born in 1769, Mary Tarpey emigrated to the US in 1853, aged 84. By 1875 she had the unique distinction of being the oldest person in Long Island, New York.[26]

While the Strokestown Park archive provides a fascinating insight into people who emigrated during and immediately after the Famine, their fate afterwards is more

THE EXODUS CONTINUES   **139**

London. Dec.r 23.
1847.

Mr. P. Mahon has to acknowledge the receipt of a Memorial, signed by G. Carton, bearing date 15th Dec.r but is not disposed to retract the warning already given, both by the late lamented Major Mahon & subsequently by himself. In consideration however for G. Carton's large family, (in the event of his Emigrating to America). Mr. P. M. will pay a sum of £10. towards the Passage of George Carton & his family, at the time of contract: the money to be paid in the event of such contract into the hands of the Ship Agent. (Mr. P. M. having made enquiry finds that Vessels sail all through

Henry Sandford Pakenham Mahon oversaw the emigration of a number of individuals, including George Carton and 'his large family' in December 1847.

STROKESTOWN AND THE GREAT IRISH FAMINE

The emigrant letter from Catherine O'Keefe to her mother at Elphin Street, Strokestown, in August 1853, illustrates some of the thoughts, fears and hopes of the Irish who left during the Great Famine.

difficult to track. For the vast majority we are offered only fleeting glimpses of their lives after leaving Ireland. An example is John Coleman, one of ninety-nine emigrants who left the townland of Curhouna during the assisted emigration programme of 1847. Having survived the crossing, Coleman made his way to New Orleans where by 1851 he is listed as being a patient in the city hospital. One of 1,100 Irish men and women, including over 20 Roscommon natives, who sought medical treatment in the hospital in 1851 alone, the ultimate fate of Coleman is unknown. Likewise, Margaret Flynn, aged 24, and her son John, aged one, who were described as 'destitute'; having survived the voyage onboard the *Virginius* in July 1847, they made their way inland to St

THE EXODUS CONTINUES   **141**

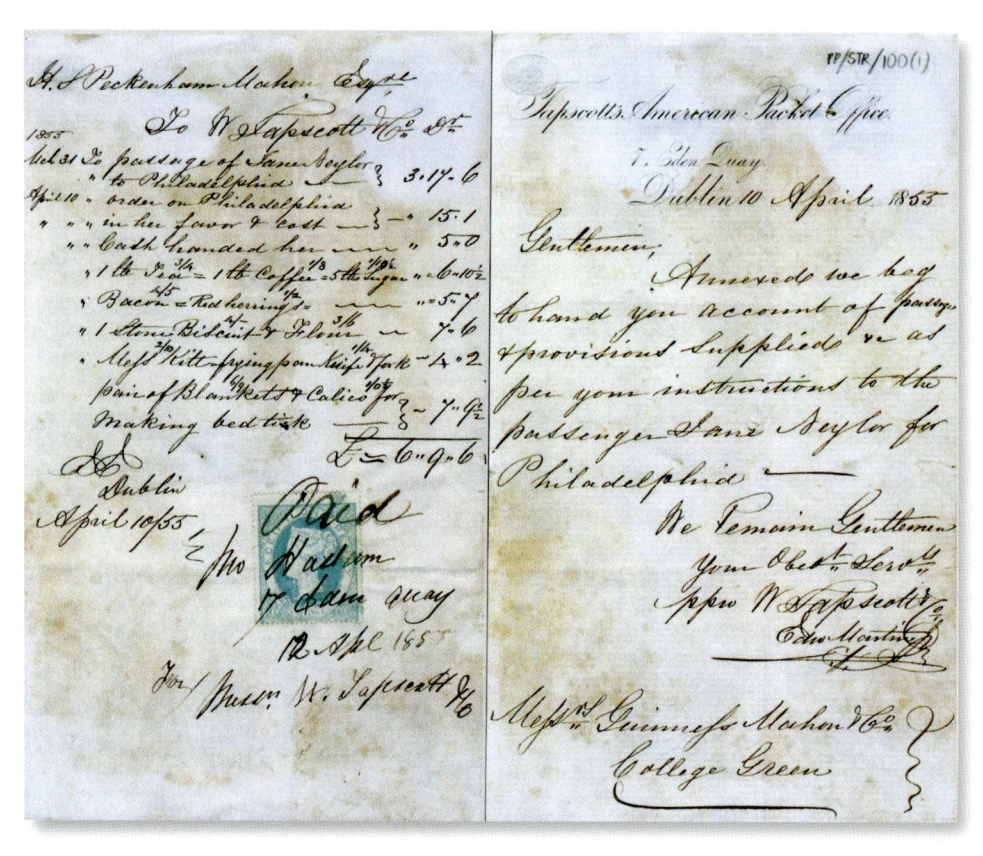

By the early 1850s, conditions onboard ships for emigrants such as Jane Neylor had greatly improved. According to the emigration agents, Tapscotts, Neylor was supplied with a generous quantity of provisions for her journey (see p.139).

John, New Brunswick, where they found shelter in the city's almshouses in 1851.[27] It was a fate that befell many more, including Anna Carlos, who died in Western Maryland in May 1851.[28] There were those with entrepreneurial zeal who adapted easily into American society.[29] Among the records of the New York Emigrant Industrial Savings Bank, for example, which had over 10,000 depositors within a decade of its inception in 1850, are the savings of Strokestown natives Michael Hayden, Ann Devine and John Brennan.[30]

The fate of most of these emigrants remains a mystery and within a generation many had lost all contact with their homeland. Advertisements in the *Boston Pilot* newspaper in the 1850s highlight the poignant search for family members who had arrived in America during or immediately after the Great Famine.[31] These advertisements illuminate the geography of emigration – and show the lost family connections that people were trying to re-establish. Many of these names correspond

Emigration case study 1: Building America

There were some remarkable success stories among Strokestown Famine emigrants. Some quickly acquired vast wealth: James Spellman, for example, within fifteen years of arriving in New York in 1846, had amassed property valued at over $5,000. Roscommon emigrants also contributed to the expansion of America's railway and canal networks, as once-inhospitable and uninhabitable lands were opened up. These included Pat Kelly (1827–1910) (*pictured*), a foreman on the railways and local politician in Wisconsin, and Patrick Hanly (1834-1920), a railroad worker in Maryland. A number of Roscommon men, including Thomas Fallon and Patrick McNamara, worked on the building of the Blue Ridge Mountain Railroad in Virginia, hailed as *the* engineering feat of nineteenth-century America. Under the leadership of the noted civil engineer, Claudius Crozet, the Blue Ridge Railroad was built through the mountain, using four tunnels, including the 4,263-foot Blue Ridge Tunnel, then one of the longest tunnels in the world. Another entrepreneur of note was Henry Higgins (1847–1929), who left Strokestown in 1851. With his brother, Thomas, he started a company providing utility work for the Baltimore–Ohio railroad. Later, he supplied gas and electric light in a number of cities in the American Midwest, and served on the board of a number of banks.

Elijah Impey (1814–66), a cousin of Edwin O'Beirne, who died of injuries sustained in the American Civil War.

with the surviving Strokestown estate archival material, allowing researchers to plot an individual's final years in Ireland before emigration.[32] They include, for example, Thomas Foley, described as a 'farmhand', who settled in Albany in 1847, and Edward Larkin from Tarmonbarry, who settled in Lawrence, Massachusetts.

There are many emigrants about whom no information is forthcoming. For example, in March 1850 Frank Coggins, his wife and four children, described as 'miserable and emaciated looking creatures', entered Roscommon workhouse. Absconding from the workhouse two weeks later with his fifteen-year-old son, Coggins made for England, before reaching America in early 1852. Having earned enough money, he sent passage tickets to the master of the workhouse for his wife and three daughters. Although the guardians consented to an allowance for the family to emigrate, no trace has been found of the Coggins family in America (see p. 136).[33]

While more research remains to be done regarding the fate of the Famine emigrants, in a number of cases their story has emerged.[34] An emigrant that we know quite a lot about is Catherine O'Keefe, thanks mainly to her correspondence in the Strokestown archive. Writing to her mother in 1853, O'Keefe outlined her new life in Melbourne, Australia, where she was surrounded by people from Strokestown and the wider Roscommon area. In full employment and leading an active social life, her journey to Australia had been pleasant and she noted that she had 'got beautiful health on sea and looked so well upon landing'. Providing a further insight into the mindset of the Irish emigrant she also noted that she 'did not see many blacks since I came here they are all white people … I must say this is a fine country but I am always speaking of going home'. O'Keefe's correspondence highlights how emigrants constantly strove to provide remittances to those who remained at home. Although settled in Melbourne, O'Keefe was full of affection for those in Strokestown, and worried as the threat of eviction still loomed.[35] Her fears for her family who remained at Strokestown were not imagined. Three years later, in December 1856, Charles O'Keefe, then a constabulary officer in county Kilkenny, received news that John Ross Mahon had finally got possession of the family home on Elphin Street. The remnants of the O'Keefe family were evicted. It was just as well, noted Charles O'Keefe, that his 'broken hearted' mother was not alive to see it.[36]

While O'Keefe's letter is exceptional in terms of detail, those interested in genealogy and local studies will have a particular interest in the Strokestown Park House Archive. Such a rich archive makes it possible to assign names to those who died, survived or emigrated during the Famine. Having identified those who emigrated, it is then possible through the use of digital databases, such as those provided by ancestry.com and others, to examine further this large exodus of people.

By the early 1850s emigration from the Strokestown estate was so widespread that agriculturalists bemoaned that there was not enough men to till the land.

THE EXODUS CONTINUES

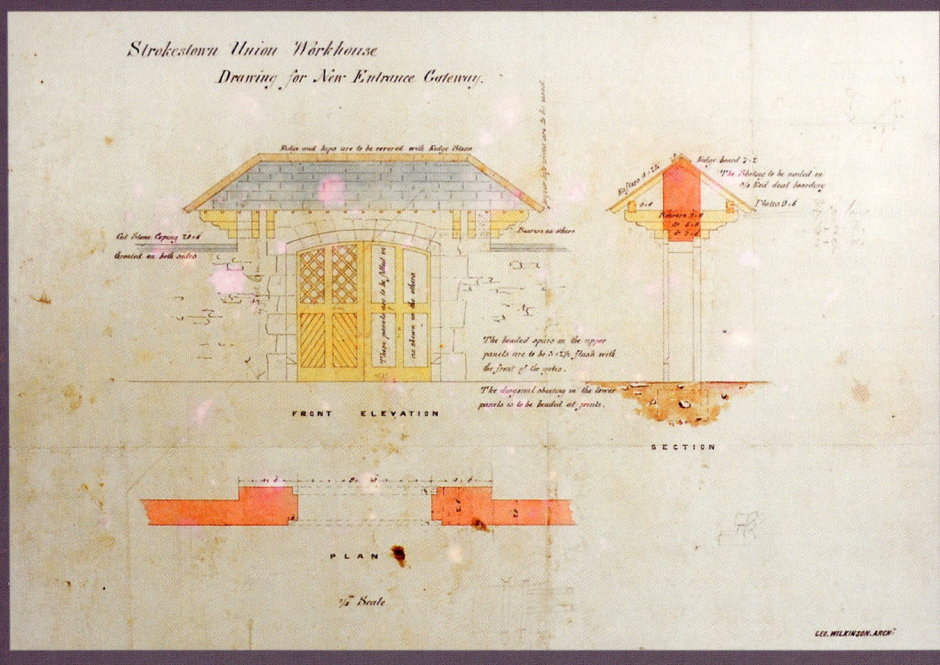

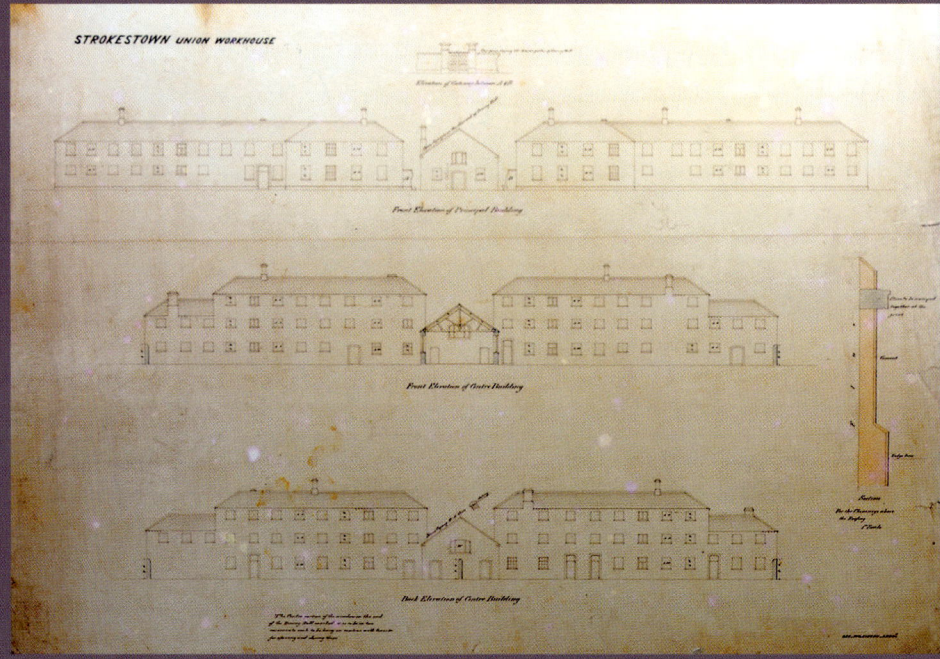

Despite objections from the inhabitants of Strokestown, a workhouse opened in the town in 1852 due to the severe overcrowding of nearby workhouses in Roscommon, Carrick-on-Shannon, Boyle and Longford. An auxillary building at Toberpatrick and a fever hospital in Churchview indicated the extent of poverty in the area.

9

Recovery and Renewal: Post-Famine Strokestown

> The ruin of your Strokestown estate at present can only be compared to the destruction of Troy.[1]

In September 1851 a large crowd gathered at Hague's hotel in Strokestown to celebrate the 'end' of the Famine. Hosted by Henry Sandford Pakenham Mahon, the party mirrored similar events across the country as landlords looked to the future with optimism.[2] Undoubtedly, those in attendance were of the strong farming and merchant class who had emerged from the Famine relatively unscathed, and in some cases had profited from the demise of others.[3] These celebrations were perhaps somewhat premature given that eviction and blight continued in Roscommon throughout the early 1850s. For Ross Mahon the celebration provided the opportunity to move forward, but plans for the renewal of the estate, and by extension the tenantry, naturally necessitated the cooperation of all concerned. As was to be expected, not everyone was enamored by the agent's handling of the estate. Pat McLaughlin, a land surveyor on the estate, highlighted Mahon's shortcomings in allowing 'bad tenants and turning away other industrious people'. The estate, according to McLaughlin, was 'strangled in the eyes of the public ... the ruin of your Strokestown estate at present can only be compared to the destruction of Troy'.[4] An anonymous letter from the same period also criticized Mahon for the fact that 'he would rather be coursing or at parties' and accused him of being little more than a 'giddy schoolboy'.[5] There was also widespread annoyance at the fact that people were 'walking about

PP/STR/211(2)

I Certify that I have Surveyd and divided that part of Curries now in the Occupation of Michael Glancey and Patt Duigman and by the assistance of Barny Duigman and John Gannon I have laid out the Same in two Equal divisions without favour affection or Malice and if necessary we will prove the same by an affermation

Jany 23rd 1850

Michael Horan

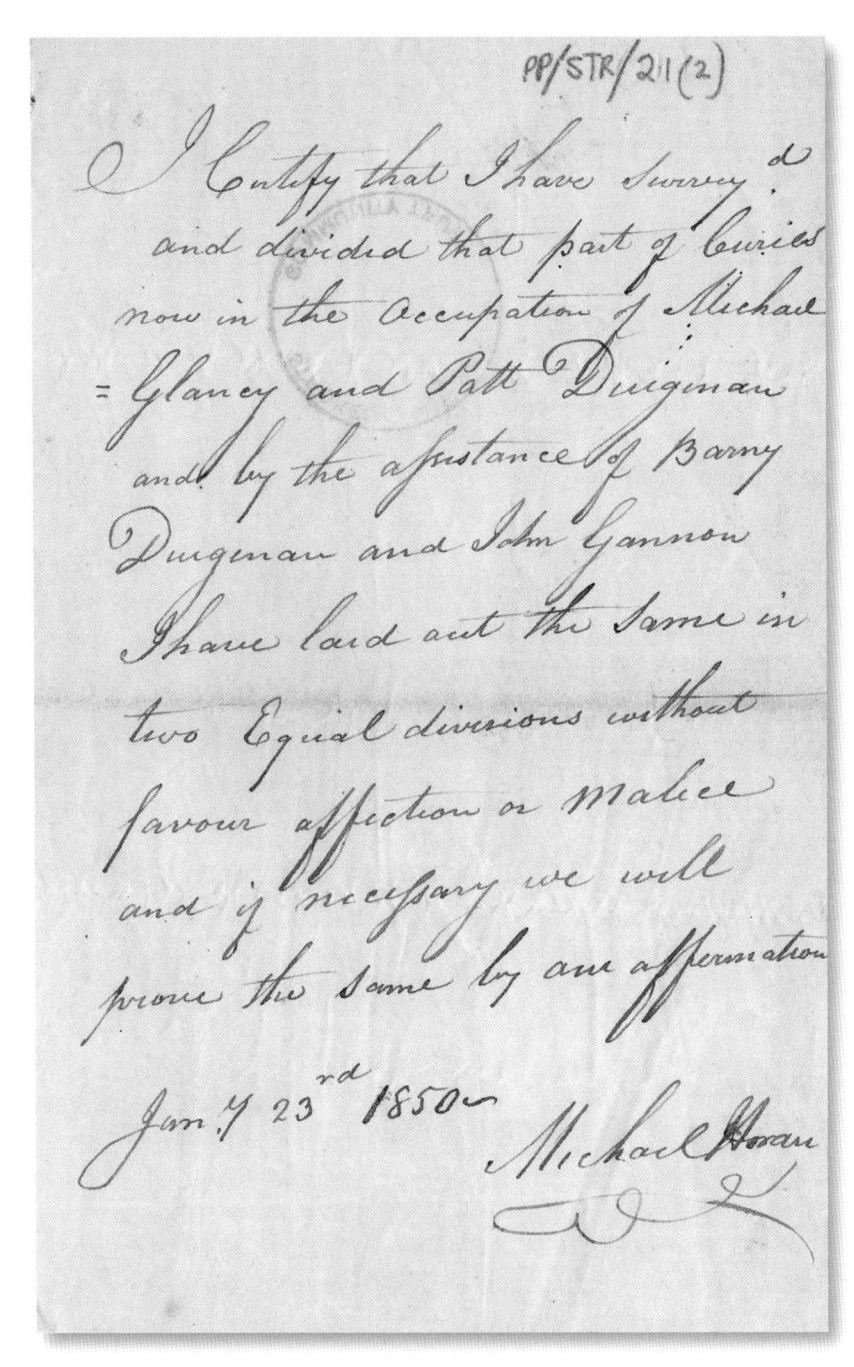

The large-scale mapping and surveying of the estate carried out in the wake of the clearances was largely the work of Michael Horan. In many instances, the surveys were undertaken to ascertain who had survived the Famine and who rented the land.

the town idle', while outside labour, in some instances from as far away as Queen's County (Laois), had been brought in.⁶

In the decades prior to the Famine, landlords had begun the move towards large-scale projects of grazing cattle and sheep, which were deemed to be more profitable than tenant-based tillage farms. By the early 1850s, the removal of thousands of tenants on the Strokestown estate meant that the way was paved for the grazier. The traveller or passerby in county Roscommon in the early 1850s could only wonder

The payment of the County Cess was another charge that landlords resented and opposed paying as the Famine wore on.

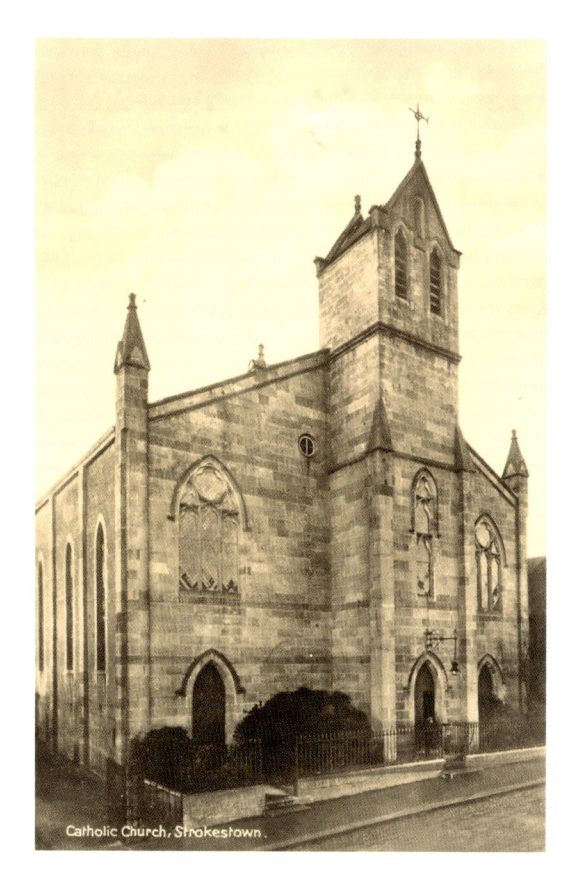

Despite the continued conflict over the murder of Major Mahon in 1847, Revd Michael McDermott requested that he be given a site to construct a new Catholic church in Strokestown in 1854. The building of the church was part of a host of improvements in the area in the 1850s.

at the vast swathe of land that was left to pasture, left idle in the hope that viable tenants would be found soon.[7] Pakenham Mahon sought to attract a new tenantry to the area, mirroring what the duke of Leinster in county Kildare, among others, had done.[8] Initially, Ross Mahon targeted progressive Scottish farmers as they were noted for their agricultural prowess and also because they might be unaware of the problems and local tension that had gone before. Strokestown had become a byword for eviction and agrarian outrage, however, and this made it less-than desirable for would-be prospectors. In 1849 a Scottish farmer visiting the west of Ireland to ascertain if it was safe for English and Scottish farmers to take up land there, commented on the depopulation of the county where entire townlands had been cleared. Such was the scale of depopulation that one landlord near Strokestown who wanted to let 150 acres could not find a tenant.[9] Many Roscommon landlords who had 'depopulated' their estates were now regretting this decision.[10]

At Strokestown, plans to redefine the estate landscape and boundaries began in earnest after the murder of Major Denis Mahon, when mapped surveys laid the foundations for a new settlement of tenants. As early as January 1848 it was suggested that these could be entirely Protestant tenants, although Ross Mahon was not convinced: 'I have not taken up with sufficient warmth a plan of his for colonizing Strokestown with Protestants' he wrote to his employer.[11] His mind was soon changed and two months later Scottish newspapers carried advertisements for the letting of over 2,500 acres on the Strokestown estate. Despite initial interested promises, Scottish tenants were not forthcoming, at least not in any large numbers, and so in April 1849 Ross Mahon

Although the growing of potatoes was not specifically prohibited as it was on other estates, in the 1850s tenants at Strokestown were encouraged to grow alternative crops, including wheat, oats and barley.

Such was the level of poaching during the Famine that a Roscommon Preservation Game Society, with Henry Sandford Pakenham Mahon as president, was established in 1854. Among the society's rules was the requirement for all dogs to be registered.

RECOVERY AND RENEWAL: POST-FAMINE STROKESTOWN   151

In the post-Famine period, Pakenham Mahon realized that for effective estate management a number of bailiffs were needed to 'police' the property and that the task was too great for the agent alone. Martin Kelly, quoted here, was one of the more active bailiffs on the estate.

made arrangements with the Dublin land agency firm, Steward and Kincaid, to secure Norfolk farmers, happy in the belief that 'others will follow I am sure'.[12] The hope was that a strong farmer, who would initially take a small holding, could later be enticed to take on a whole townland.[13] The problem was that so many tenants had been cleared that these Norfolk farmers alone were not sufficient to farm the estate. It was then that Irish Protestant farmers were enticed to Strokestown, a plan to which the embattled Revd Joseph Morton agreed: 'I quite agree with you that it would be a great object to get some Protestant tenants & I hope we shall succeed in doing so'.[14]

152 STROKESTOWN AND THE GREAT IRISH FAMINE

> PP/STR/64(21)
>
> Shanbally
> Thomas Roberts Esqr 22nd March 53
>
> Honrd sir I have to state there not many holdings on the property even the most respectable Tenants on the property has under tenants on their holdings and I do not know how to act until I hear from your Honour as to burning there is none of the arable land burned on the property unless bog or bottom land on the of McDonoug & and higgins in arm there is an acre of bottom land let and prepared for burning your Honour may act with them as you please

The Famine did not eradicate the problem of subdivision and, although expressly forbidden from doing so, even 'the more respectable tenants' did it well into the 1850s.

Emigration case study 2: The American Civil War

It has been estimated that as many as 200,000 Irishmen fought in the American Civil War (1861–5), with about 180,000 in the Union Army, and 20,000 in the Confederate forces. Among these were a significant number who had fled the horrors of the Great Irish Famine. Emigrants from Strokestown took part in a number of battles in the conflict, including three Fallon brothers who fought for the Confederacy: Thomas was killed at the Battle of Piedmont near Staunton, Virginia; James was captured at the battle of Gettysburg and imprisoned at Fort Delaware in 1863, while John was captured and imprisoned at Camp Chase, Ohio in 1864. Others, like Michael Flynn (1834–1906), who lost an eye, and Pat Flanagan, who lost an arm, survived the war. Another story connected to the Civil War concerns the fate of Strokestown native, Edwin O'Beirne (*pictured*). Although not a soldier, O'Beirne was working at the home of Logan Dysart of Jackson, Missouri, a Southern sympathizer, when it was set on fire by pro-Union forces. When attempting to quench the flames O'Beirne was shot and killed. His cousin, Elijah Impey, also from Strokestown, was described as a 'bitter and uncompromising Southern man', and later died of injuries sustained in the war.

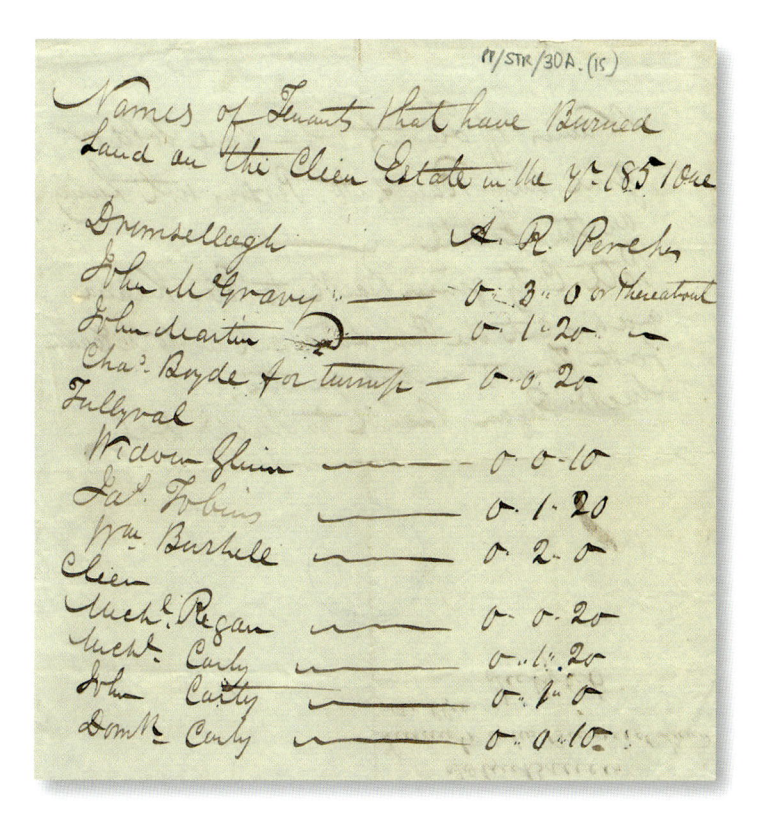

In the pre-Famine period, tenants had regularly burned the land as a means of preparing for the next crop. This practice was prohibited by Pakenham Mahon and those found to have violated the rule could be ejected from the estate.

The intensive mapping and surveying of the estate was, in many cases, to ascertain who had survived the Famine and what land now lay idle.[15] Often it was not known if the tenants or persons listed on leases were even alive. For example, before serving ejectment proceedings, William Roe, the estate solicitor, advised that 'you must find out if Luke Hanly or Michael Hughes or either of them are alive, if they are you must serve a copy of ejectment on each of them; if only one is alive serve it on him'.[16] Indeed, some areas had not been visited by estate officials since the mid-1840s.[17] In 1851 an amusing incident involving two tenants named O'Beirne and Keogh underlined this. They had sent in a proposal to remain on land at Lecarrow, despite the fact that they were not entitled to be there in the first place.[18] The surveying of the estate was once again seen by tenants as a gross intrusion, who saw it solely as a means of recovering arrears. In 1851 William Laughlin, a large farmer at Castlecoote, noted that 'it is extraordinary ... the richer the man the more particular he is in exacting his due'.[19]

With the middlemen removed, or stripped of much of their property, the way was now paved for the redistribution of land. At Cloonfad More, for example, Patrick

DRAINAGE.

Acts 5 and 6 *Victoria, Cap.* 89—8 and 9 *Victoria, Cap.* 69—9 *Victoria, Cap.* 4—10 and 11 *Victoria, Cap.* 79—16 and 17 *Victoria, Cap.* 130—and 18 and 19 *Victoria, Cap.* 110.

DISTRICT OF STROKESTOWN,
In the County of Roscommon.

NOTICE is hereby given that Printed Copies of the Draft of the Final Award of the Commissioners of Public Works in Ireland, with respect to "THE DISTRICT OF STROKESTOWN," made pursuant to the provisions of the above-mentioned Acts, have been deposited in the Office of the Clerk of the Peace for the County of Roscommon.

And Notice is further given, that all Persons are at liberty to inspect the same. And all Persons who may desire to lodge objections to said Awards are hereby required to lodge the same at the *Post Office, Strokestown*, addressed to

The Secretary,
Board of Public Works,
Dublin,

on or before the 15th day of *April* next.

And Notice is hereby further given, that the said Commissioners will hold a MEETING of all Persons interested, at the

COURT-HOUSE, STROKESTOWN,

on *Thursday*, the 22nd day of *May* next, at the hour of 12 o'clock, noon. And they will then and there proceed to hear any objections which may be lodged to said Award, and examine into the matter of any such objections which shall be so lodged, and hear all such proper evidence as may be offered to them in respect thereof, and will make such alterations (if any) in the said Award as they shall think fit, and settle and sign such Award.

By Order of the Commissioners of Public Works in Ireland,

EDWARD HORNSBY,

Drainage was promoted on a large scale in the post-Famine period and advice was sought on how best to proceed in this regard. The estate work accounts indicate that several hundred men were employed at drainage in the 1850s.

Browne, the bishop's brother, who had once been the dominant middleman, was retained but reduced to a holding of just over sixty-five acres. In some instances middlemen were simply replaced by a better class of tenant and there is evidence to suggest that many were allowed to continue the practice of subdivision. These strong tenants acted as a buffer from poverty and could also be relied on to provide support when called upon by the landlord. It appears likely that these tenants were handpicked although Michael Horan, the estate surveyor, attested that he had divided up holdings on the estate without 'affection or malice'.[20]

The reorganization of the estate also necessitated enlarging the size of individual holdings; Ross Mahon believed that for tenants to prosper going forward no holding should be less than nine acres. Having identified land that could now be consolidated, Ross Mahon, with his team of officials, also began to radically alter the farming practices of tenants. Those who remained were instructed by the agriculturalist to change their husbandry and such advice was now a requirement for remaining in tenancy on the Strokestown estate. To improve the quality of cattle on the estate several new breeds were brought in from England, Scotland and the Continent. These included Dutch heifers and a bull, to which tenants could bring their cows on an annual basis.[21] Estate officials were also sent to Scotland to procure the best breeds of sheep.[22] Moreover, the growing of potatoes as a staple crop was discouraged, although not prohibited as on other estates.[23] Large parts of the estate required drainage and schemes to encourage new methods of draining were implemented. Those with knowledge of such schemes, including Richard Irwin, championed the Lancashire sod drain, which, when properly done, was deemed to be the best and cheapest mode of draining.[24] To finance the project, Pakenham Mahon secured a £1,000 loan, under the Land Improvement Scheme, from the Office of Public Works.[25] Tenants were also encouraged to build new slated houses and abandon the practice of living in cabins.[26] Those in a position to construct new houses were provided with plans and estimates for doing so. A typical plan given to tenants was for a house thirty-six feet long by thirteen feet wide, which required six pairs of rafters, and cost £3 12s. to build. As a further incentive blue bangor slates were bought.[27]

Improvements did not end there. An examination of the Strokestown work accounts for the years 1847–51 indicates that more than 600 men were at work on the estate, which no doubt greatly reduced local hardship. The jobs performed included ploughing, jobbing, stable work, fencing, gardening and making hay.[28] Tenants were also encouraged to supplement their incomes, as they had done prior to the Famine, by establishing cottage industries, using as capital remittances sent from America and other locations.[29] Tenants were curtailed in their activities and their

LAND IMPROVEMENT.

> OFFICE OF PUBLIC WORKS,
> 25th of October 1850
>
> SIR,
>
> I am directed by the Commissioners to request that you will, with as little delay as possible, fill up and return the enclosed Form, showing the quantity of Work executed, and the amount paid, under your Loan of £ 1000 the Certificate for the *third* Instalment of which was issued so long since as the 16th August 1849
>
> I am,
> SIR,
> Your obedient Servant,
>
> *E. Hornsby*
> Secretary
>
> Henry S. P. Mahon Esq
> Strokestown House
> Strokestown

Drainage and other improvements were financed by a £1,000 loan from the Office of Public Works under a land improvement scheme.

conduct was expected to mirror the more respectable farming class. For example, the keeping of greyhounds and other dogs was prohibited as a means of counteracting the widespread poaching that had severely depleted game and other animals.[30] Ross Mahon and his team were also keen to replenish forests and plantations, presumably after much theft during the Famine. In the early 1850s over 7,000 trees were planted in the immediate vicinity of the town, including 2,500 scotch fir, 500 larch, 500 Norway spruce and 500 Dutch elm.[31] The planting of trees mirrored Pakenham Mahon's wish

County Roscommon.

SPRING ASSIZES, 1855

Baronies of Roscommon and Ballintobber North:

LISTS of APPLICATIONS approved of at the several Presentment Sessions held in and for the respective Baronies of Roscommon, and Ballintobber N. in this County, for the following works &c, and the said Sessions were afterwards adjourned as set fourth for the purpose of receiving and opening such sealed Tenders and Proposals as shall be delivered for the execution of all such works. The specifications relating thereto may be seen at the Office of the County Surveyor. All Forms of Tenders may be had at this Office previous to the said Adjourned Sessions respectively.

Barony of Roscommon.

At Strokestown 11th December, 1854. Adjourned to Tuesday 2nd January, 1855.

1—To repair 150 perches of road from Frenchpark to Strokestown, between Thomas Rush's house at Killina, and James Warnock's contract at Doonmoroho. Not to exceed 3s. 6d. per perch.

3—To repair 60 perches of road from Elphin to Richmond harbour, between Patt Mannion's house at Lismakeegan, and Charles Moraghan's house in Cloonshannagh. Not to exceed 2s. 6. per perch.

4—To repair 150 perches of road from Roscommon to Rooskey, between the turn of the road near Luke Owens's house in Lismeby, and John Connor's house in Aughadaugan. Not to exceed 2s. 6d. per perch.

6—To repair 100 perches of road from Elphin to Fuerty, between the Widow Carney's house in Rathmore, and the mearing of the barony of Ballymoe, at Grange. Not to exceed 3s. per perch.

7—To repair 200 perches of road from Strokestown to Roscommon (by Cloonfinlough). Not to exceed 2s. 6d. per perch.

8—To lower 15 perches of a Hill on road from Strokestown to Roscommon, (by Cloonfinlough,) between the church of Strokestown, and the bridge of Cloonfinlough to the townland of Cloonslannard. Not to exceed £9.

10—To repair 104 perches of Footpath on road from Strokestown to Boyle and Elphin, between Mr. Lynch's house in Elphin, and where the present Footpath terminates. Not to exceed 1s. per perch.

13—To keep in repair for one year 200 perches of the road from Frenchpark to Drumsna, commencing at the turn to the windmill, as far as said perches will extend, towards Smith hill, to the street of Elphin. Not to exceed 2s. 6d. per perch.

12—To keep in repair for 3 years 652 perches of the road from Strokestown to Boyle and Carrick-on-Shannon commencing at Michael Tiernan's haggart gate and ending at the cross roads at Mr. Arthur O'Conors gate. Not to exceed 1s. per pech.

14—To keep in repair for 3 year 420 perches of the road from Roscommon to Elphin commencing at the bridge of Ballyoughton, and ending at the cross roads of Shankill. Not to exceed 6d. per perch.

15—To keep in repair for 3 years 832 perches of the road from Strokestown to Jamestown commencing at the cross roads of Corkeena and ending at the Ballintubber North barony, at Foxwood. Not to exceed 4d. per perch.

16—To keep in repair for 3 years 953 perches of the road from Strokestown to Frenchpark (by Cloonyquin,) commencing at the cross roads of Cloonyquin and ending at Mr. Irwin's gate at Raheen. Not to exceed 6d. per perch.

17—To keep in repair for 3 years 1626 perches of the road from Elphin to Strokestown (by Cloonahee) commencing at the cross roads at Smithill and ending at the cross roads of Creta. Not to exceed 6d. per perch.

18—To keep in repair for 3 years 312 perches of the road from Roscommon to Boyle (by Ballyroddy,) commencing at the cross roads of Carnamore. Not to exceed 6d. per perch.

19—To keep in repair for 3 years 560 perrhes of the road from Strokestown to Drumsna and Carrick-on-Shannon, commencing at the cross roads of Cloonygarvin, and ending at the boundary of the barony at Feeragh. Not to exceed 1s. 6d. per perch.

22—To keep in repair for 3 years 1134 perches of the mail coach road from Strokestown to Longford commencing at the cross roads of Scramogue and ending at the mearing of Ballintubber South barony, at Foorish. Not to exceed 2s. 6d. per perch.

23—To widen the bridge of Clashaganny, and build fence walls, in the townland of Clashaganny and Grange. Not to exceed £50.

Barony of Ballintobber North.

At Kilmore, Tuesday 12th December, 1854. Adjourned to Wednesday 3rd January, 1855.

1—To repair 100 perches of road from Strokestown to Carrick-on-Shannon, to the Village of Muckanagh, between John Gillooly's house in Grange, and Mr. Balf's gate in Muckanagh. Not to exceed 2s 6d. per perch.

2—To repair 200 perches of road from Elphin to Richmond harbour, and Longford, between Larkfield gate, and the bridge of Buncocca. To be pointed out by Captain Hanly. Not to exceed 3s. per perch.

3—To repair 100 perches of road from Jamestown to Richmond harbour and Killashee, between the cross roads of Duffslattagh, and the mearing of the barony of Roscommon at Cardrummin. To be pointed out by Mr. Balfe. Not to exceed 3s. per perch.

5—To repair the battlements and protecting walls on both sides of the bridge, on the road from Strokestown to Drumsna, on the mearing between the townlands of Clogher and Dargan. Not to exceed £10.

6—To repair 213½ perches of Footpath on the North side of the mail coach road from Jamestown to Drumsna, between the bridge of Jamestown, and the town of Drumsna. Not to exceed £20, half to be leviel off the County at Large.

7—To keep in repair for 3 years 371 perches of road from Rooskey to Lanesboro, commencing at the cross roads of Tully and ending at Edward Burke's house in Ballyfeeney. Not to exceed 6d. per perch.

10—To make 80 perches of an earth fence on the west side of the road from Strokestown to Rooskey, between Mary Roddy's house in Tully, and the cross roads of Glen. Not to exceed 6s. per perch.

11—To scour, widen, and deepen perches of drains at the new road from Rooskey to Tarmon in the townland of Cloonahill and Kilvarry.

12—To repair 100 perches of road from Strokestown to Tarmonbarry between the old road and To be pointed out by Captain Hanly. Not to exceed 3s. per perch.

All which I Certify,

M. SHARKEY,
Secretary to the Grand Jury, County Roscommon.

Roscommon, Secretarys' Office, 18th December, 1854.

Despite being an absentee landlord, Pakenham Mahon was anxious that Strokestown would recover from the Famine, and actively encouraged improvement, as witnessed in the applications to the Roscommon Spring Assizes in 1855.

to have Strokestown laid out as one of the finest towns in Ireland, one that would be admired by all visitors. Strokestown was not altogether forgotten by the family after the Famine, and Pakenham Mahon began to spend longer periods visiting, often up to two months at a time. His visits generally prompted an air of excitement about the town and in advance of a visit to the estate in 1853, tenants were requested to have their houses white-washed and 'the place itself made as orderly as possible'.[32]

There was also a growing realization that better educated tenants would be more likely to cooperate with estate management. As a result, education was promoted on a number of levels by the landlord. Indeed, every effort was made by Thomas Roberts and John Ross Mahon to ensure that the tenantry who remained after the Famine would be properly educated. New schools were built at Northyard, Culliagh and Curries, where tenants were employed in drawing stone and other materials for use in the construction. Books published by the Society for Promoting the Education of the Poor of Ireland formed libraries at these new schools. One of the more interesting developments on the estate in the post-Famine years was the building of the new Roman Catholic Church in Strokestown in 1854.[33] Obviously no longer hindered by the controversy of 1847, Revd Michael McDermott petitioned Roberts for help in this matter and highlighted 'the immediate necessity of enlarging our chapel to accommodate the large congregation … in consequence of the late union of the two parishes'. He further outlined the limitations of the present church and the need 'to build on a new site'.[34] Despite the ongoing animosity between priest and landlord, McDermott was allowed to build the church.

The promotion of industry was also encouraged at Strokestown, although several attempts to provide employment failed. Enquires were made to the Irish Beet Sugar Company about the possibility of establishing a sugar factory at Strokestown, while the arrival of prosperous tenants, including Mr Wapole, a Quaker, who intended to build a mill, were broadly welcomed.[35] It was also hoped that the Society of Friends (Quakers) would start a model farm at Strokestown and bring several of their congregation there. However, as in other towns, there appears to have been a reluctance in certain quarters to accept the Quakers and to conduct business with them.[36]

Despite efforts at improvement, Strokestown still retained the appearance of devastation following the levelling and clearance of houses throughout the Famine. Martin Doyle, a surveyor for Griffith's Valuation of Ireland, commented that 'the markets and fairs are the chief support of the town as there are neither mills nor manufactories'. In particular, Doyle singled out the shopkeepers of the town as being part of the overall problem as they 'realized high profits, keep inferior articles, get high prices, and are able to make higher rents here than in larger towns'.[37] Writing in 1856, the county Roscommon landlord, Lord Crofton of Mote Park, described Strokestown as having a 'wretched, miserable and deserted appearance'. In addition, Crofton stated that while:

> there are certainly two or three good fairs held in the town because the stock is good and well attended to, the town itself bears the appearance of an absentee proprietor.[38]

The continued absenteeism of the family naturally hindered the recovery of the estate. Lord Crofton believed that Pakenham Mahon would never return to Strokestown because he 'could not think of asking his wife to return to the scene where her father was so brutally murdered and where she knew there would be cognizance of many of the inhabitants'.[39] Responding to such negative comments by Crofton and others, Ross Mahon staunchly defended the area, and, more importantly, his management of the estate, noting that 'Strokestown is a rising instead of decaying neighbourhood'.[40] He was supported by the under-agent Thomas Roberts who was said to be 'really annoyed at Lord Crofton's statement of it being in a state of dilapidation'.[41] While there was an obvious bias on the part of Crofton, not least because of his objection to the advance of the railway line to Strokestown, there was an air of truth to it. In the short period 1845 to 1851, more than 32 per cent of the population of county Roscommon had died or emigrated, and on the Strokestown estate there were 6,000 fewer people by the time the Famine ended.[42]

> Carrumoneen
>
> Sir pardon me to say that within those years past I have lived in the utmost danger of my life in consequence of my neighbour Michl. Nerheny who is brother in law to Andrew Connor whose character I need not describe this Michl Nerhany has now in his house Connor's wife & children as a terror to all his Neighbours And has receivd from Connor a considerable portion of the money collected for the conspiracy of the Major's life tis evident too that he has Connor's arms together with letters of communication from him where ever he is, besides Nerheny kept a Shebeen house previous to the Major's death wherein Connor & his associates often drank together And after the perpetration of the Barbarous deed Shewed the greatest Symptoms of Joy which many can testify &c &c &c
>
> N.B. the within Statement I purposed often to inform your Honor of, but fearing my life if publickly known
>
> I have the Honor to be your humble Servant
> James Neheny
>
> To J. A. Mahon Esqr
> Strokestown
>
> Carrumoneen
> May 15th 1847

> To Thomas Corry Esqr
>
> Sir a few of your tenants were Innocently Convicted and the Delinquents are returned although had Absconded the Country & is now returned your honour is solicited to Receive Informations privately & have the said Offenders debarred its a pity to Innocent persons persecuted and others the Defaulters at liberty plunder & give the Neighbourhood a bad name when nearly rid of bad Characters &c
>
> Anne McGuire

Tenants were sometimes happy to inform the landlord or his agent of the actions and character of their neighbours, friends and families, as these letters from James Neherny and Anne McGuire reveal.

10

Conclusion: Social Memory and Culpability

In 1981, the 300-year Pakenham Mahon family's connection with Strokestown ended. After eight generations of Pakenham Mahon residence in Strokestown, Olive Hales Pakenham Mahon, then aged eighty-seven, moved to a nursing home in England where she died later that year. As was her wish, she was buried in Strokestown, not in the family vault in the demesne, but in the local cemetery.[1] With the Troubles raging in Northern Ireland, her son, Nicholas Stuart Hales Pakenham Mahon (1926–2012), then a serving member of the British Army, was advised that it would be unsafe to return to Strokestown.[2] Although the family had long enjoyed cordial relations with the local community, they were continually haunted by the memory of the Great Famine, in particular the murder of Major Denis Mahon and the fate of those who died at sea or at Grosse Île in 1847. Over subsequent generations a conscious effort was made to emphasize the Irish lineage of the family and their longevity at Strokestown, perhaps as a means of countering the memory of eviction and clearance that characterized the 1840s. In 1947, for example, at the coming-of-age of the aforementioned Nicholas, his father William Stuart Hales Pakenham Mahon cited the family's long and friendly connection with the people of Strokestown:

> Why is the family still here in the same house after such a period of time? I can tell you the reason. It is because of the people of Strokestown. It is their friendship. Hard work

After the murder of her father, Major Denis Mahon, Grace Pakenham Mahon vowed never to return to live at Strokestown. It wasn't until the 1890s that the house was again occupied, then by her son, Henry (pictured here with his family c.1900).

> and neighbourliness that has enabled this family and your families ... even through the ups and downs of a disturbed history ... the old books of a hundred-and-fifty years ago show many of the same names as I see on the books today and many of your families have lived here for as long or longer than the Mahons ... doubtless some of them went to battle against the Danes with Mahon ... one therefore feels that this is a family party to congratulate Nick on reaching twenty-one and to wish him luck and long life in the future.[3]

Even in this address, the Famine must have loomed large in the thoughts of the audience. So pivotal were the events of the 1840s that later incidents were not remembered with the same clarity or animosity. For example, the fate of female

The Strokestown estate was not unique in that agents, bailiffs, rent warners and other officials were regularly accused of 'feathering their own nests' but certainly many profited during this time of severe want, as this letter from Laughlin Beirne to Thomas Roberts in 1852 shows.

paupers sent from Strokestown workhouse to Canada in the 1850s or of 100 'paupers' sent from Strokestown workhouse to America in 1883 is largely forgotten. Refused entry to New York, it is not known what became of these emigrants.[4] Social memory is selective in nature and over time the murder of Major Denis Mahon and the evictions of the 1840s were presented in different ways. In 1952, for example, a Strokestown native recalled how the murder of Major Mahon 'was a case of mistaken identity. Nobody would harm a hair on his head, as he was much beloved by the people,

CONCLUSION: SOCIAL MEMORY AND CULPABILITY   165

Built to accommodate just over 600 people, by the end of its second year in 1851, Strokestown workhouse had over 850 'inmates', evidence of the continuing poverty and destitution.

especially his own tenants'.[5] Speaking in Dáil Éireann in 1962, Fine Gael TD for Monaghan, James Dillon (1902–86), reiterated these sentiments, arguing that Major Mahon was 'a young idealist, honourable and generous, and not at all the kind of man who merited murder'.[6] Local folklore gathered in the 1930s and 1940s noted how the local community enjoyed 'the use of the demesne at will, a privilege that many have taken advantage of'.[7] Other accounts, however, present a complete opposite viewpoint, and portray the Pakenham Mahon family as the villains of the Famine narrative. In evidence to the Bureau of Military History in 1954, Patrick Mullooly of Kiltrustan, a veteran of the Irish War of Independence, spoke about the Mahon family and their association with Strokestown:

> The Mahon family of Strokestown Demesne were the landlords of that district then. Years previously especially during the Famine years they oppressed their tenants so cruelly that one of the family, a Major Mahon, was shot dead ... Even his coat of mail availed him little protection.

166 STROKESTOWN AND THE GREAT IRISH FAMINE

> Thos Roberts Esq
>
> Sir it appears very strange to me the tennants who has not paid their rents the office day after your trouble coming to convince them that they would not send down the rent by a post office order and each of them able to pay their rents it shews a great jelousy to the others who would wish to get the same indulgence some of them to say next harvest we will pay him a years rent with the crop, if I had instructions to destrain such persons cattle I would not allow them but the same time the others got who attend very respectable and paid their rents, John healy should pay instead of bying meal or oats for the rent saying I will pay after the fair Con O'roarke should also pay at the worse the holding his cattle is on in Ardsallaghmore, Mr McCormeck also if Mr madden was at home I know he would remit a letter of credit to you McGrath & Connor should pay or let those people forget the abatemt Send me instructions how I will manage those, and also about the farm if cattle will be taken on it and in my oppenion it would be better not to let any stock on it the land would look better
>
> I am Sir your humble & obet Servt Michl Murray
>
> unpaid
> Mr Madden
> Mr Sharkey
> John Connor
> Jno Magrath
> Con. O'roarke
> Cathrine O'roarke
> Patt McCormeck
> John Healy
>
> let me hear from you and if persons writes for time you know what to do

It was obvious to estate officials that many tenants refused to pay rent throughout the Famine despite being in a position to do so. Refusing to pay on the grounds that others were doing likewise, many stubbornly persisted in not paying, even to the point of eviction.

> As a result two men named respectively Hasty and Cummins were hanged in Roscommon town. A third man named Gardiner escaped to the USA but returning after a lapse of 21 years sought out his comrades' graves and there knelt and prayed. He then paid a visit to Major Mahon's grave and spat on it. The incident was reported to the English Authority of the day and again Gardiner was on his keeping, but again succeeded in reaching the USA, in those days known as 'The land of the Free'. He never could dare again visit his native place and now his last resting place is beside the waters of the Rappahanock.[8]

Owing to their knowledge of the tenantry, bailiffs like John Bruen of Cleen were seen as an integral part of the estate administration. After the Famine, Bruen and others simply replaced the middlemen and themselves sublet the land.

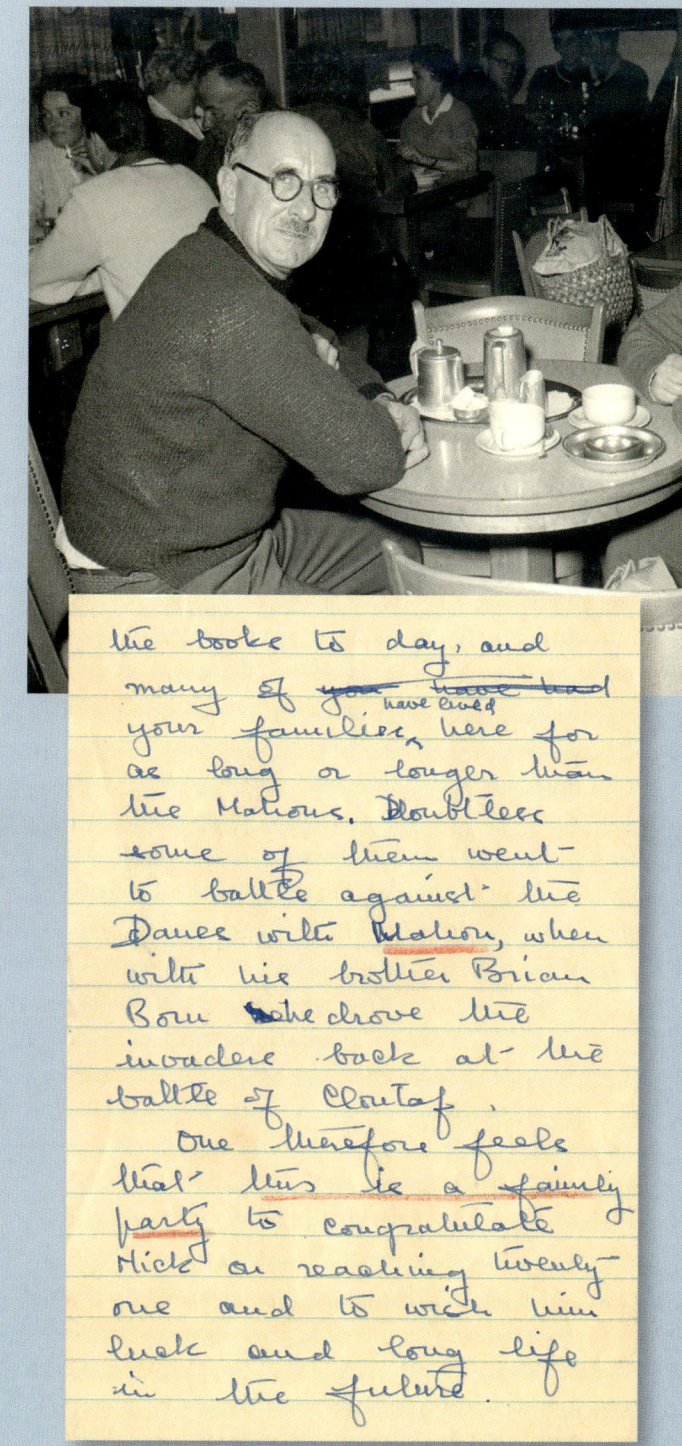

In 1947 Major Stuart Hales Pakenham Mahon, speaking at the coming-of-age of his son, Nicholas, highlighted the long association that the family had enjoyed with the people of Strokestown. The Major (pictured above with his wife, Olive) made no mention of the Great Famine or the assisted emigration scheme that had occurred 100 years earlier.

CONCLUSION: SOCIAL MEMORY AND CULPABILITY **169**

> H.S. Pakenham Mahon Esq. to Charles Maguire
> Clerk of Strokestown Petty Sessions — Dr.

		£ s d
January	To one Information as to the burning of the House at Lacken	0 "1" 0
9 March	To Four Informations made by the Care takers Against Lieutenant Sidebottom	0 "4" 0
Do	To Two Pair of Summonses against Same	0 "1" 0
12	To Two Pair of Notices to put out weekly Tenants	0 "2" 6
12	To Three Pair of Summonses against said Tenants	0 "1" 6
14	To Information Frank Bunnan Informant	0 "1" 0
14	To ~~Copying Four Informations against Mr Sidebottom~~	
14	To ~~Copying two Pair of Summonses agt~~	0 "1" 0
20	To one order for Possession	0 "1" 0
20	To one Pair of Notices served on the returning officer before giving up possession	0 "0" 6
Do	To one habere &c	0 "2" 0
20	To Two Convictions against Mr Sidebottom	
		£0.15.0

To Thos Roberts Esq. 28 March 1851

Received the amount of the above bill from Thos
Roberts Esquire this 28th day of March 1851
viz Fifteen shillings on
account H.S. Mahon Esq. Charles Maguire

Unlike pre-Famine Ireland where local communities were unwilling to offer information on crime and other matters, people were more than willing to give information during and after the Famine. The document above shows the expenses paid to Charles Maguire for bringing convictions against a number of tenants.

Unsurprisingly, the murder of Major Denis Mahon continues to loom large in social memory and as Robert Scally contends 'nothing of greater importance' ever happened in Strokestown.[9] The demise of Major Mahon is remembered in different guises locally and forms the basis for folk and ghost stories.[10] In addition, the murder has also featured in several works of fiction, with Mahon the mould for the evil and capricious Irish Famine-era landlord. One recent work of fiction included the passage 'then Major Dens Mahon was on the road again, spuds dripping from his wagon and spilling on the road'.[11] Descriptions such as this have fuelled the belief that Mahon was a 'particularly nasty piece of work', although one recent author contends that it was somewhat ironic that 'Mahon was turned on by the very tenants he tried to assist at Strokestown'.[12] There is little surviving testimony of how the Pakenham Mahon family themselves recalled the murder and the events of the 1840s. However, one interesting account provided by Nicholas Hales Stuart Pakenham Mahon, on display in the same room at the Irish National Famine Museum as the alleged gun which shot Major Denis Mahon, sheds some light on the matter. About this sorry chapter in Strokestown's history, Major Mahon's great-great grandson commented:

> Being a descendent of Major Mahon who died as a direct result of the Famine, I put on record my sorrow for all the others, particularly the families living on the Strokestown estate, who died and suffered in Ireland's greatest tragedy. He [Major Mahon] was left with the alternatives of seeing his tenantry starve around him or encouraging many of them to emigrate, the cost of their passage to Canada being paid by him.[13]

While it is certainly true that the emigration schemes and the clearances caused considerable unrest, which contributed to the murder of Denis Mahon, social memory, if left untested, can hide many of the complexities as to how the Famine played itself out at a local level. The content of the Strokestown Famine archive indicates that there are still major questions to be answered in relation to the greatest social calamity in modern Irish history. How widespread and effective were local efforts to alleviate the plight of the impoverished? How did the local community react to the clearance of thousands of people, and who benefited from these clearances?

In the early 1850s, the Irish antiquarian George Petrie, while travelling through the countryside, noted the 'awful, unwonted silence' about the Famine period.[14] In later generations, however, those who broke silence attached particular censure to the land grabbers, shopkeepers, merchants and others who had profited from the catastrophe. As one respondent to the Irish Folklore Commission commented, 'several people would be glad if the famine times were altogether forgotten so that the cruel doings of their forebears would not again be renewed and talked about by their neighbours'.[15] It was these people that William Carleton had in mind when he wrote in 1847:

> There is to be found in Ireland, and, we presume, in all other countries, a class of hardened wretches, who look forward to a period of dearth as to one of great gain and advantage, and who contrive, by exercising the most heartless and diabolical principles, to make the sickness, famine and general desolation which scourge their fellow creatures, so many sources of successful extortion and rapacity, and consequently of gain for themselves.[16]

At Strokestown, the behaviour of the local community with regard to the provision of relief, the scramble for land and the treatment of women and children challenges any casual assumptions about evil landlords and blameless tenants. Such behaviour may suggest why people were anxious to forget what occurred during the 1840s and 1850s.[17]

The Strokestown archive provides a fascinating insight into the behaviour of the local community during the Famine, in particular those who were anxious to gain access to land. As a result of eviction and emigration, land at Strokestown became a much sought-after prize. Large farmers were anxious to get some of the land that was being carved up on the Strokestown estate.[18] Indeed, for some, as a respondent to the Irish Folklore Commission noted, 'their only ambition was to come by land'.[19] At Strokestown they were facilitated in their efforts by bailiffs, rent warners and other estate officials who were accused of corruption. It was even claimed that the local constabulary were also implicated: 'if you appeal anything to the barrack they will swear that black is white for him. There is not a man in the barrack that has not a stock of heifers' noted one anonymous letter in 1851.[20] There were others too who were anxious to acquire new premises and land.[21] They included Revd James Nally of Tarmonbarry and Revd John Hanly of Kilgafin, both of whom sought to be considered for land from which their parishioners had been evicted.[22] Others looked

Kilmacough	Repr. Major Mahon	" Cathein	9
Farymount	Mr. Lyster	Patt Hanly	44
"	"	Wife Biddy	35
"	"	" Thomas	12
Carraward	"	Catherine Carroll	55
Clooncah Hines	M. McCausland Esq.	Michl. McGrath	15
Aughalahard	"	Patt Donlon, apt.	14
Sheehaun Hughes	Peter McKeogh Agent	Luke Geoghegan	6
Farymount	Mr. Lyster	Catherine Gormly	13
Tuam	Richd. Irwin Esq.	John Leheny	40
Farymount	Mr. Lyster	Patt Gormly	6
"	"	" Margt.	2
"	"	" James	12
Clooncah Hines	M. McCausland Esq.	Margt. McGrath	16
Aughalahard	"	Daniel Maguire	18
Farymount	Mr. Lyster	Thomas Hanly	14
Sheehaun Morton	Peter McKeogh Agent	Tho. McCormick	20
Tuam	Richd. Irwin Esq.	Biddy Madden	15
Lacken	Repr. Major Mahon	Mary Farrell	55
Cloonshee Connor	Roderick O'Connor Esq.	Anne Mulligan, maid	33
"	"	" James	1
Farymount	Mr. Lyster	Mary Gormly	14
Kilnalosset	H.S.P. Mahon Esq.	Thos. Broderick	9
"	"	" John	7
Trilacroghan	John Ireslan Esq.	Martin Kenny	14
Tuam	Richd. Irwin Esq.	Mary Morgon	50
"	"	Nabby Madden	20
Cappagh	M. McCausland Esq.	Anne Kerns	15

The numbers of women and children at Strokestown abandoned in the workhouse during the Famine raises awkward questions about culpability. While it may be argued that these women and children survived by entering the workhouse, their experience of abandonment surely affected them for the rest of their lives.

CONCLUSION: SOCIAL MEMORY AND CULPABILITY 173

The Famine and memory

In the 1850s, when the Irish artist and antiquarian George Petrie (1790–1866) travelled through Ireland, he noted the 'awful, unwonted silence' that existed about the Great Famine. In the period immediately after the Famine many were reluctant to talk about what had happened. In recent times this has come to be described as a Famine 'muteness', which caused 'a deep blow to the psyche' of the Irish people. Undoubtedly, there were huge psychological scars on the Irish population, on those who remained and those who emigrated. Although the sesquicentenary commemoration of the Famine in the 1990s produced a plethora of scholarly publication and research, much remains to be understood about the calamity. The meaning, causes and consequences of the Famine continue to be debated. The Irish National Famine Museum at Strokestown leads the way in providing a platform to educate, discuss and disseminate research on Ireland's worst social catastrophe. The Famine Museum also has the potential to become an international focal point for a wider consideration of the experience of contemporary famine and global hunger.

for neighbours to be removed, particularly those who had caused trouble in the past. In the highly contentious townland of Dooherty, John Boyd was among a number of people who begged 'the clearance of the cabins ... as he wants it very much'.[23] Moreover, just as Helen O'Brien has illustrated in the case of Toomevara, county Tipperary, large farmers and others were happy to assist bailiffs in the tearing down of huts that were illegally built by evicted tenants, while some actively helped in the removal of their own relations. Some people even used the Major Denis Mahon murder trial as a means of settling scores and a number of people gave false information to police. For example, Luke Lyons maintained that in September 1847 Martin Mulligan had lent him his gun and told him to shoot Major Denis Mahon. Countering these claims Mulligan maintained that because he had taken part in the levelling of Lyons' house, revenge was now being sought.[24] Other harrowing accounts emerge of the greed of neighbours, family and friends. For example, in 1848 a widow at Strokestown complained that having buried her husband and two children, her father-in-law now wanted to evict her and that she had 'not a bit nor sup' to feed her remaining children.[25] Vying for land, neighbours could be remorseless in their actions. In 1852 Luke Murray of Cordrummin was evicted from the estate after he had been found guilty of the burning of a neighbours house in a dispute over access to land.[26]

Unsurprisingly in these circumstances, there was little resistance shown to eviction and no collective action was taken against the clearances of 1848 and 1849. Even the serving of over 300 notices to quit by process servers, Charles Carlos and John Cooney, in 1849 met with little opposition. It was a similar scenario when Thomas Williams was paid 5s. for levelling eight houses in one day at Scramogue, near Strokestown, where as many as forty people were ejected.[27] In other parts of the country, such as county Monaghan, evicted tenants reacted by cutting off the tails of cattle and attacking the houses of those who had gained possession.[28] At Strokestown there appears to have been a great silence on the whole matter. It was the considered opinion of some evicted tenants that those who could pay rent were forcing out those who could not.[29] In many ways the actions of the Strokestown community mirrored Hugh Dorian's account of the Famine in the Fanad peninsula in county Donegal:

> Friendship was forgotten, men lived as if they dreaded each other, every one trying to do the best for himself alone, and a man would rather deny the goods he possessed than make it known that he had such or that he was improving in the world.[30]

There was no shortage of people willing to inform on the behaviour of their neighbours, particularly those who owed rent or who stood in the way of them acquiring a holding. In May 1849 John McCann, a 'watcher', provided an in-depth survey of the Tarmonbarry portion of the estate, including the number of acres tenants had planted in wheat, oats, potatoes and the number of cows, heifers and houses that they owned.[31] McCann feared for his own safety and wished to remain anonymous in supplying information.[32] Although a team of 'watchers' were in place on the estate, very often information received by the agent came from other sources. In particular, tenants were willing to inform on those who possessed 'hard money' with which they purchased conacre, cattle and other household materials.[33] In December 1849, for example, Pat Gibbons informed the agent that his neighbour had three stacks of oats and had £5 in money, despite his claim that he could not pay the rent.[34] The elderly and infirm were also targeted; neighbours vied to be given possession of the holdings of elderly neighbours.[35] As James Donnelly Jr notes, this type of behaviour would have been very painful for subsequent generations, and so was repressed.[36] Just as Famine survivors were reluctant to admit that they had received relief, either on the public works, in workhouses or in soup kitchens, others were not keen to mention the acquisition of land.[37]

As the Famine wore on, the attitudes towards the provision of relief is also revealing.[38] At Strokestown several shopkeepers argued that they should not be expected to look after the welfare of the poor, 'for if they did there would be expensive dealing'.[39] Likewise, the objection towards the construction of a workhouse in the town said much about the changing public attitude:

> The houses of Mr Egan of Strokestown are well situated for an auxiliary house but the inhabitants of the town seem very much against there been taken, not wishing the paupers to be brought into the town for fear of the disease.[40]

Ultimately, the delay in acquiring a site for a workhouse in Strokestown had a detrimental effect on those most in need. Prior to its opening in 1852 a significant number of Pakenham Mahon's tenants sought shelter and relief in Roscommon workhouse.[41] While the clearances on the estate made it necessary to construct a workhouse at Strokestown, so too did the abandonment of women and children. In a revealingly large number of cases, young children and women were abandoned as family members emigrated. They included Maria Hanly, aged eleven, who was abandoned by her father; Winifred Hannelly, who with four children was deserted by her husband Darby, and Catherine and Pat Connor, aged ten and eight, who were left in the workhouse by their mother who 'eloped' to England.[42] Other cases highlighted the plight of children whom their parents wished to be rid of. In 1851, for example, Michael Bolan, aged nine, was denied access to the workhouse as his mother had remarried a Mr Keating, who, it seems, was of considerable means. Occasionally, abandoned children – like two girls named Conlon – described as 'poor distressed creatures', were offered assistance, but there appears to have been so many that not all could be accommodated.[43] While in some cases family members did return or sent remittances, for the majority they did not. This surely caused repressed memories and a reluctance to speak about the Famine among later generations.

Issues such as culpability remain contentious in relation to the Great Irish Famine. Many landlords endeavoured to cull and eliminate their Famine papers; in doing so they may have done the local community a favour, as culpability for many actions would be erased. At Strokestown, it has suited many that the Pakenham Mahon's were depicted in the social memory of the Famine as the despoilers of the people, and this has distorted the picture of what actually happened during the Famine. It is interesting then, when accessing the Famine at a local level, not what is remembered but what was forgotten, deliberately forgotten in many cases. Speaking in Boston at the National Famine Commemoration in 2012, President of Ireland, Michael D. Higgins, reminded us that there is not a single narrative of Ireland's greatest social catastrophe and that:

> It is necessary to revisit, revise and include much that has been forgotten or perhaps deliberately avoided in a great silence amongst the survivors at home and abroad. We must be open to amending what we have taken as the iconic event, the master narrative, and add in some missing bits, drawing on the new scholarship.[44]

The Strokestown archive allows us to do just that.

The gun which shot Major Mahon

On loan from Mrs Delia Finneran, Lisgobbin, Kilrooskey

Among the artefacts contained in the Irish National Famine Museum is the gun that is alleged to have shot Major Denis Mahon. On loan from Mrs Delia Finneran, Lisgobbin, Kilroosky, county Roscommon.

Postscript:
The Making of the Irish National Famine Museum

> Strokestown presents a hugely rich potential for multiple, interlinked narratives, which could for example embrace ideas of consumption, production, deprivation, and sustainability, either in terms of yesteryear, today, or tomorrow. Indeed, given contemporary prognostications about global food shortages and climate change, it might be argued that these narratives, both historical and contemporary, have never been more relevant. Strokestown has the potential to be the most exciting house in Ireland.[1]

In May 1994 the Irish National Famine Museum opened at Strokestown Park House. Using the documents contained in the Strokestown archive, the museum aimed to tell the story of the Great Irish Famine, while also highlighting the fact that global hunger was still a major problem in the twentieth century. Speaking at the opening ceremony, the museum's first patron, President Mary Robinson, commented that 'more than anything else, this Famine museum shows us that history is not about power or triumph really so often as it is about suffering and vulnerability'.[2] Historian Peter Gray was among many early admirers of the Famine museum and believed

Olive Pakenham Mahon, the last owner of Strokestown, pictured during the First World War.

that it was 'sober, didactic and educational, without being oppressive', while the novelist Nuala O'Faolain, although she had grown up indifferent to houses such as Strokestown, noted that it was 'better to embrace such legacies as we've got. Visiting Strokestown is some such tentative embrace'.[3] For journalist Kevin Myers there was no more appropriate place than Strokestown to establish the museum and for him the archival material was key to this, displaying the 'resurgent symbols of death'.[4] Others saw the museum as offering a 'genuine attempt at cultural re-connection' with Irish-America.[5] Government officials were equally impressed with the museum; county Wicklow Dáil Deputy, Liz McManus, claimed that:

> the method used by the initiator of the project it seems to be a far more appropriate way to interpret our past. It presents the evidence of different viewpoints – indeed

> sometimes conflicting viewpoints — in a way that respects the modern person's intelligence and leaves the questions open for deliberation and judgment by individual observers. Through a babble of voices and not through one, inevitably restricted or even moribund view, do we gain a better insight into our past.[6]

Plans for the museum had long been in gestation, with one reporter calling it the 'longest pregnancy in history'.[7] A significant sum was spent in the development, with matching European funding, for what was quickly described as the most challenging and revolutionary museum in Ireland. Before the museum had even opened, Strokestown was awarded the Ford Irish Conservation Award in 1992 for 'the scope and the enlightened energy with which it is being pursued'.[8] Then-Taoiseach Albert Reynolds believed that Strokestown was a 'marvellous example of a resource being preserved to provide visitors with a view to both sides of Irish society in the time of the Famine'.[9] While comments like these were obviously very welcome there was some degree of pride among those involved in the project that the funding for Ireland's first Famine museum had been provided by the charity of the Westward Group.[10] According to Declan Jones, managing director of Westward's property division,

Strokestown House at the turn of the twentieth century.

The marriage of Olive Pakenham Mahon and Major Stuart Hales in December 1921.

the restoration of the house and the opening of the museum 'was by no stretch of the imagination a viable commercial undertaking' and although Strokestown Park continues to make an annual deficit, the board of Westward Group are determined that the story as presented in the house, museum and gardens will continue.[11]

The opening of the museum, coming as it did three months before the beginning of the Northern Ireland Peace Process, offered hope that the complexities of the Famine could now be properly addressed and that historians and the general public would tackle the many issues that had been deliberately avoided in the past. It also came a year before the official state commemoration of the Great Famine began in 1995. The Irish National Famine Museum played a crucial role in awakening the Irish people (and indeed those further afield) to commemorate the events of the 1840s. Moreover, many of the community initiatives to remember the Famine in 1995 and after were inspired by events at Strokestown. For the museum's then-curator, Luke Dodd, who was instrumental in its establishment, the opening meant 'that the estate has assumed

The Strokestown estate in the twentieth century

Under the 1903 Wyndham Land Act, much of the Strokestown estate was transferred to the tenantry, with the Pakenham Mahon's retaining just over 300 acres. Unlike many of its counterparts it was spared destruction in the revolutionary period, largely because it was occupied by the East Yorkshire Regiment during the War of Independence (1919–21). However, the personal fortunes of Olive Pakenham Mahon mirrored those of so many other Irish gentry families during the Great War. Within a period of just five months she had been married, became pregnant (a daughter would be born in early 1915) and made a widow, when her husband, Captain Edward Stafford-King-Harman, was killed on 6 November 1914 at Ypres. In 1921 she married Major Stuart Hales and returned to Strokestown where she remained until 1981. After purchase by the Westward Group, Strokestown House was opened to the public in 1987; the Famine Museum was established in 1994; the walled gardens reopened in 2001 and the woodland walk was restored in 2011. Strokestown continues to attract more than 50,000 visitors annually.

(*Above*) Part of the Irish National Famine Museum, which uses original documents from the archive to tell the story of the 1840s.

(*Left*) President of Ireland, Mary Robinson, first patron of the Irish National Famine Museum, arrives for the official opening in May 1994 accompanied by Jim Callery.

a new and meaningful function in an Ireland that's completely different from the one that originally produced it'.[12] For both Dodd and Jim Callery, education over tourism was the agenda, and all efforts were made to negate the image of victimhood.[13] In doing so they were also hoping to 'consciously reintegrate Strokestown into Irish history'.[14]

From the outset the Famine museum at Strokestown has had its critics. For many, the location of Ireland's first museum dedicated to the memory of the Great Famine was misplaced. In 1994 Terry Eagleton, for example, described it as 'a postmodern museum in a Palladian setting, bereft of all central narrative, skewing one image against another in a parody of conventional museum practice ... installed in a stately pile whose owners did their best to deepen the disaster'.[15] For others, the location of the museum, being as it is juxtaposed to the 'Big House', was 'grimly appropriate'.[16] While attitudes have since softened, one recent observer has remarked that the luscious surroundings of the Big House, park and gardens at Strokestown are in stark contrast to depredation and starvation that the Famine museum attempts to portray.[17] More recently, it has been suggested that the 'the sombre and informative' museum 'acts as a kind of atonement for the behaviour of Major Denis Mahon' and his kin during the Great Famine.[18]

(*Above*) President Michael D. Higgins, patron of the Irish National Famine Museum, speaking in Strokestown at the official reopening in May 2013.

(*Left*) President of Ireland, Mary McAleese, second patron of the Irish National Famine Museum, with her husband Dr Martin McAleese and Jim Callery in Strokestown House, 2008.

In May 2014 Strokestown was chosen as the venue for the National Famine Commemoration in recognition of the role that the Irish National Famine Museum plays in educating and informing on the Great Famine.

Regardless of such criticism, the continued stream of visitors to the Famine Museum, more than 50,000 people annually, is testament to the foresight of its founders and all those who continue to oversee its development. However, there are many challenges ahead. Writing in 2012, Terence Dooley cautioned that

> Strokestown Park and the Irish National Famine Museum have survived because of the financial commitment of the Westward Group and a small but dedicated staff. However, it is unlikely that the Westward Group will be in a position to continue to finance the museum without some form of state assistance. The present economic downturn should not be a pretext to avoid providing this; there is already a growing realization that tourism is central to the reinvigoration of the Irish economy.[19]

At the National Famine Commemoration, An Taoiseach, Enda Kenny TD, unveiled a memorial wall that displays the names of the 275 families (1,490 people) who emigrated from Strokestown in May 1847.

While the salient facts of the Great Famine are well known, the museum, principally through the use of archival material, continues to allow access to the forgotten world of the Famine. A recent renovation, officially unveiled in May 2013 by the current patron of the museum, President Michael D. Higgins, allows visitors the chance to examine and interpret the largest collection of Famine-related material on display anywhere in the world. In recognition of the role played by the Irish National Famine Museum, in May 2014 Strokestown Park was chosen to host the annual National Famine Commemoration. On the twentieth anniversary of the opening of the Famine Museum, it was evidence of the importance of the site and also recognition of the work that has been ongoing there. The Irish National Famine Museum continues to provide a platform for the many forgotten voices of the 1840s, eloquently contained in the voluminous Strokestown Park archive.

Notes

Introduction

1. See, for example, Fintan O'Toole, 'Bleak House', *Irish Times,* 14 May 1994; Luke Dodd, 'Heritage and the "Big House": whitewash for rural history', *Irish Reporter,* 6 (1992), p. 10.
2. Terence Dooley, 'The Big House and Famine memory' in John Crowley and William Smyth (eds), *Atlas of the Great Irish Famine* (Cork, 2012), p. 625.
3. 'Petition of the Cloonahee tenants' (SPHA).
4. Christopher Ridgway, 'Making and meaning in the historic house' in Terence Dooley and Christopher Ridgeway (eds), *The Irish country house: past, present and future* (Dublin, 2011), pp 228–9.
5. In the 1950s a sizable amount of papers from Strokestown Park House were transferred to the National Library of Ireland, and now form the Pakenham Mahon collection. Until recently it was believed that much of the material in the Pakenham Mahon papers in the National Library were concerned mainly with the eighteenth century. However, research on the collection reveals that a significant number of documents relating to the Famine period are contained in the Pakenham Mahon papers, which compliment the Strokestown archive and thus should be consulted simultaneously. According to Ainsworth's report (NLI, no. 425), the collection came to Olive Pakenham Mahon in 1959 and had formerly been at Apley Park, Bridgenorth, Shropshire. Among a number of items that have 'disappeared' and are not part of either the Strokestown collection or the Pakenham Mahon papers in the NLI are an 1812 journal belonging to Major Denis Mahon; a journal belonging to Grace Pakenham Mahon detailing her tour of France and Italy in 1847 and other Famine-related material.
6. For example, the dearth of Famine-related material can be seen in the Rosse (Birr) and Conolly (Celbridge) estate collections. See A.P.W. Malcomson (ed.), *Calendar of the Rosse papers* (Dublin, 2007), Patrick Walsh and A.P.W. Malcomson (eds), *Calendar of the Conolly papers* (Dublin, 2010).
7. This facility is an exciting collaboration between the Office of Public Works and Maynooth University.
8. This work has been overseen by archivists Roisín Berry, Ciara Joyce, Nicola Kelly and Susan Leydon.
9. Quoted in *Irish Independent,* 14 Nov. 2008.
10. The archive highlights the plight of Mary Lenehan of Elphin Street, Strokestown, an ancestor of President McAleese, who received meal as part of relief measures in the town in June 1846. See 'List of names of those persons relieved with meal gratuitously on Monday 22 June 1846' (SPHA).
11. Other studies that examine the impact of the Famine on individual landed estates include Gerard Lyne, *The Lansdowne estates in Kerry under the agency of W.S. Trench, 1849–72* (Dublin, 2001); Anthony Doyle, *Charles Powell Leslie II's estates at Glaslough, county Monaghan, 1800–1841* (Dublin, 2001); Helen O'Brien, *The Famine clearance in Toomevara, county Tipperary* (Dublin, 2010); Ciarán Reilly, *John Plunket Joly and the Great Famine in King's County* (Dublin, 2012) and Tom Crehan, *Marcella Gerrard's Galway estate, 1820–70* (Dublin, 2013).
12. While this book provides an introduction to the archive, a forthcoming publication will examine how the Great Famine played itself out in this area in much greater detail.

Chapter 1: 'Towards the Abyss': Strokestown on the Eve of the Famine

1. Skeffington Gibbon, *The recollections of Skeffington Gibbon from 1796 to the present year, 1829; being an epitome of the lives and characters of the nobility and gentry of Roscommon; the genealogy of those who are descended from the kings of Connaught; and a memoir of the late Madame O'Conor Don* (Dublin, 1829), p. 153.
2. For more on this see C.J. Woods, *Travellers' accounts as source material for Irish historians* (Dublin, 2009).
3. Gibbon, *The recollections of Skeffington Gibbon*, p. 153.
4. John O'Donovan, 'Letters containing information relative to the antiquities of the County of Roscommon, collected during the progress of the Ordnance Survey in 1837' (Typescript, Roscommon County Library, 1931), p. 47.
5. 'Statement of Patrick Mullolly, Kiltrustan, Strokestown, county Roscommon' (NAI, Bureau of Military History Witness Statement, no. 1086).
6. For more on the family see The O'Conor Don, 'Ballintubber Castle, County Roscommon', *Journal of the Royal Historical and Archaeological Association of Ireland*, 4th series, 9:78 (Jan.–Mar. 1889), pp 24–30. See 'Conveyance by Edmond Dillon of Ballynamully, esq., to Nicholas Mahon of Elphin, esq., for £617 5s. of the castle, town and lands of Ballynamully and of other denominations, 25 Jan. 1662' (NLI, PM papers).
7. Gibbon, *The recollections of Skeffington Gibbon*, p. 7. For another and more recent interpretation of the family history see *Sunday Independent*, 27 May 2012.
8. See, for example, Anthony Ward, 'Strokestown Park', *Roscommon Association Yearbook* (1986), p. 67; *Leitrim Observer*, 28 May 1988; *The Tribune*, 12 July 1987.
9. Baron Hartland, Strokestown to Francis Evans, Rathcormick, county Cork, September 1804 (NLI, XI P.928).
10. 'Notes prepared for the coming-of-age speech of Nicholas Hales Pakenham Mahon, 1947' (SPHA).
11. Susan Hood, 'The landlord-planned nexus at Strokestown, county Roscommon: a case study of an Irish estate town, c.1660–c.1925' (PhD, University of Ulster, 1994), pp 46–7.
13. For a detailed breakdown of landholding in Ireland during this period see www.downsurvey.tcd.ie.
14. Indeed, as late as the 1840s a dispute over the fair of Strokestown was settled using legal documents which had been granted to the Mahon's by King Charles II (SPHA).
15. The best authority on this remains Hood, 'The landlord-planned nexus at Strokestown, county Roscommon'. Today, Strokestown is said to boast the widest street in Europe; built by Thomas Mahon, he planned the town so that it would have a street wider than the Ringstrasse in Vienna.
16. Nicolas Mahon died, on 10 October 1680, aged 60.
17. 'Manuscript notes in Olive Pakenham Mahon's hand, dated 1930' (SPHA).
18. Hood, 'The landlord-planned nexus at Strokestown', p. 119.
19. More work was carried out on the internal portion of the house in the 1760s when chimneys and wine cellars were added. See NLI, PM papers, MS 10, 157 (2).
20. Arthur Young, *A tour in Ireland: with general observations on the present state of the kingdom made in the years 1776, 1777 and 1778, and brought down to the end of 1779* (reprinted Shannon, 1970), pp 214–20. Connor was head gardener at Strokestown between 1781 and 1783. See James Donnell to Maurice Mahon, 1 July 1788 (NLI, PM papers, MS 10,086 (1)).
21. 'Estimate for Maurice Mahon for building a gothic gate and wall to go across the town of Strokestown (1790–99)' (NLI, PM papers, MS 10, 158 (2)).
22. Young, *A tour in Ireland*, p. 216.
23. See, for example, *Morning Chronicle*, 13 Jan. 1819.
24. Isaac Weld, *Statistical survey of the county of Roscommon* (Dublin, 1832), pp 329–30.
25. Ibid., pp 330–1.
26. The year before her death, for example, she spent £127 on a new grand pianoforte and £295 on upholstery and drapes for the parlour in her Dublin town house in Merrion Square. See William Stodart to Lieutenant General Mahon, 5 June 1830 (SPHA).
27. 'Copy charge submitted by Denis Mahon, to the Committee of the estate of the lunatic, Lord Hartland, 25 Apr. 1845' (PRONI, D/1550/46). See also Mahon estate accounts (NLI, PM papers, MS 10, 153).

28 *Pigot's, Directory, 1824*, p. 217.
29 Samuel Lewis, *A topographical dictionary of Ireland*, 2 vols (London, 1837), ii, p. 581.
30 This local unrest was recorded in the diary of Sir Alexander Crichton, a Scottish physician and landowner, who criticized the 'beastly inn' at Strokestown and the habit of people crying 'murder' in the middle of the night and on all occasions. See 'Diary of Sir Alexander Crichton, 1829' (PRONI, MIC 613/1).
31 *The recollections of Skeffington Gibbon*, p. 153.
32 Denis Mahon (1787–1847) was born on 12 March 1787, and was a major in the 9th Lancers. In September 1822 he married Henrietta, daughter of Henry Bathurst, bishop of Norwich. He was definitely not simply the seven-acre holder of land as some have observed in the past.
33 A letter in the Strokestown archive in relation to information for *Burke's peerage and baronetage*, dated 28 Nov. 1840, states that due to paralysis, Revd Maurice Mahon was unable to manage his affairs, and so now resides at Strokestown House with the guardian of his person and property, Denis Mahon. In 1841 Denis Mahon was elected High Sherriff of county Roscommon.
34 See, for example, 'Receipt for items bought by Major Denis Mahon from Peter O'Connor, Sligo, 25 July 1843' (NLI, PM papers, MS 10,101 (2)). See also Maurice Conry to Denis Mahon, 10 Somerset Street, Portman Square, London, 13 Mar. 1839 (SPHA).
35 For example, on the Tarmonbarry portion, the bailiff is recorded as going over the tenants' properties in December 1839; June 1840; July 1844 and July 1846.
36 Memorandum book relating to tenants of the Mahon estate at Tarmonbarry, Co. Roscommon, 1839–46 (NLI, PM papers, MS 9,740). The estate was surveyed and bailiffs, including the notorious John Robinson of Farnbeg, were instructed to include the name of every tenant, the size of their holding, the quantity of materials and 'every piece of timber in each house'. See Major Denis Mahon to Thomas Conry [n.d.] 1843 (SPHA).
37 Denis Mahon to Tom Conry, 11 Jan. 1844 (SPHA).
38 'Notice of the Strokestown Loan Fund, 1839' (SPHA). Those acquiring assistance from the loan fund included landholders, dealers, shoe makers, tailors, weavers, smiths, nailors, hatters, carpenters, sawyers, wheelwrights, turners, coopers, masons and butchers.
39 See, for example, the petition of Michael Farrell to John Ross Mahon, 12 Nov. 1847, which refers to the damage caused in 1839 (SPHA).
40 Correspondence of the Strokestown Loan Fund, May 1839 (SPHA).
41 *Devon Commission*, p. 605.
42 See, for example, the letter of Maria Payton, Baltimore, US, to Margaret Flanagan, Strokestown, 15 July 1841 (SPHA).
43 At Strokestown it was estimated that about 150 people sought seasonal work elsewhere of whom about 50 went to England. See *First report from His Majesty's commissioners for inquiring into the condition of the poorer classes in Ireland*, with appendix (A.) and supplement, 1835 (369), p. 39.
44 *First report from His Majesty's commissioners for inquiring into the condition of the poorer classes in Ireland*, supplement to appendix B, part 1, 1835 (369), p. 12.
45 Ibid., p. 61.
46 Edward Wakefield, *An account of Ireland, statistical and political*, ii (London, 1812), p. 128.
47 Pakenham Mahon map books (NLI, MS 16 M 15).
48 Thomas Conry to Baron Hartland, 10 Dec. 1831 (NLI, PM papers, MS 10,099 (2)).
49 Bishop of Elphin, Power Le Poer Trench to Mr Gregory, 5 Aug. 1813 (NAI, SOCP, 1538/20). See also Michael Huggins, *Social conflict in pre-Famine Ireland: the case of county Roscommon* (Dublin, 2004), pp 27, 74–5.
50 *FJ*, 18 & 21 July 1832.
51 *Abstract of the police reports of some of the principal outrages in the counties Tipperary, Clare, Limerick, Leitrim and Roscommon in the year 1845*, HC, 1846, 710.
52 *Atlas of the Great Irish Famine*, p. 15.

53 Surprisingly, the British newspapers provide the best background to some of these pre-Famine crimes. See, for example, *Bristol Mercury*, 10 July 1841.
54 *Derby Mercury*, 4 Oct. 1843.
55 *London Standard*, 10 Apr. 1844.
56 *Bath Chronicle and Weekly Gazette*, 27 June 1844.
57 Ibid.
58 *Carlisle Journal*, 11 Jan. 1845.
59 *FJ*, 27 Mar. 1845.
60 Ibid., 3 Apr. 1845.
61 *Ipswich Journal*, 12 Apr. 1845.
62 *Kentish Gazette*, 8 Apr. 1845. Other reports noted that much of county Roscommon and Leitrim were overrun with bandits. See, for example, *Ipswich Journal*, 12 Apr. 1845.
63 Huggins, *Social conflict*, p. 43.
64 *FJ*, 9 Jan. 1845.
65 Rental of the Strokestown estate, 1843 (SPHA). See also 'A list of tenants who are to be ejected at Kildalogue, 30 Nov. 1841' (SPHA). The tenants included Pat Kelly, Arthur Goodman, Pat Bowens, John Doyle, John Kenny, Pat Moor, Michael Beirne, John Gibbons, Ed Kealy, John Healy, James Finnegan and Bryan Finnegan.
66 *FJ*, 9 Apr. 1845.

Chapter 2: 'The Poorest Peasantry on the Face of the Earth': Early Relief Efforts, 1846–7

1 'Circular letter from J. Irwin, secretary of the relief committee for the parishes of Ballintobber, 3 Nov. 1846' (SPHA).
2 *London Standard*, 17 Nov. 1845.
3 'Resolution of the inhabitants of Termonbarry, 1822' (NLI, Mahon of Castlegar papers, MS 47,844 (1)).
4 For the first reports of the blight see *Farmers' Gazette*, 13 Sept. 1845. Rotten potato fields in Castlebellingham, county Louth, for example, were among the first to herald its arrival.
5 See, for example, Dr J. Cowell, Philipstown, King's County to Relief Commissioners, 8 Nov. 1845 (NAI, RLFC, 2/Z15408). See also Thomas P. O'Neill, 'The organization and administration of relief 1845–52' in R.D. Edwards and T.D. Williams (eds), *The Great Famine: studies in Irish history, 1845–52* (Dublin, 1956), p. 210.
6 See, for example, P.M.A. Bourke, 'The scientific investigation of the potato blight in 1845–6', *Irish Historical Studies*, 13:49 (1962), pp 26–32.
7 *FJ*, 8 Nov. 1845.
8 *RJ*, 18 Oct. 1845.
9 See, for example, *FJ*, 10 Oct. 1845.
10 *RJ*, 30 Mar. 1846.
11 Robert Stokes to Major Denis Mahon, 11 Apr. 1846 (NLI, PM papers, MS 10,101 (4)).
12 Major Denis Mahon to Relief Commissioners, 30 July 1846 (NAI, RLFC, 3/1/4917).
13 See, for example, Major Denis Mahon, Strokestown House to Thomas Conry, 28 June 1846 (SPHA).
14 *London Standard*, 29 Jan. 1846. See also *Kentish Gazette*, 26 May 1846. Pouring scorn on these assassins the *Kentish Gazette* praised the liberality of Browne who had endeavoured to look after his tenants.
15 *Morning Chronicle*, 5 Feb. 1846.
16 *RJ*, 19 Sept. 1846.
17 James Gray to Thomas Roberts, 30 Mar. 1848 (SPHA).
18 J.C. Walker, Secretary OPW, to William Stanley, 3 Oct. 1846 (NAI, RLFC, 3/2/25/58).
19 *FJ*, 21 Oct. 1851. Indeed, during the board of works drainage of several lakes in the Strokestown area, several antiquarian finds were uncovered, prompting the visit of members of the Royal Irish Academy.
20 Ibid.

21   Major Denis Mahon to Tom Conry, 28 June 1846 (NLI, PM papers, MS 10,101 (5)).
22   *Preston Chronicle*, 19 Dec. 1846.
23   *London Standard*, 15 Jan. 1846
24   See, for example, *Carlisle Journal*, 13 June 1846; *Norfolk News*, 6 June 1846.
25   Revd McDermott to Tom Conry, May 1846 (SPHA).
26   James Gray to Thomas Roberts, 30 Mar. & 14 July 1848 (SPHA).
27   *Report of Her Majesty's Commissioners of Inquiry into the working of the Landlord and Tenant (Ireland) Act, 1870, and the acts amending the same*, 1881 [C.2779] [C.2779-I] [C.2779-II] [C.2779-III], pp 657–8.
28   Revd Michael McDermott to the Relief Commissioners, Dublin Castle, 12 June 1846 (NAI, RLFC, 3/1/3168).
29   William Parks, Drumsna to Thomas Roberts, n.d. [1852?] (SPHA).
30   *RJ*, 29 Aug. 1846.
31   *RJ*, 6 June 1846.
32   Major Denis Mahon to Richard Pennefather, Dublin Castle, 26 June 1846 (NAI, RLFC, 3/2/25/57).
33   Major Denis Mahon to Relief Commissioners, 14 July 1846 (NAI, RLFC, 3/1/4289).
34   Quoted in Peter Duffy, *The killing of Major Denis Mahon: a mystery of old Ireland* (New York, 2007), p. 140.
35   *RJ*, 8 Aug. 1846.
36   Ibid., 26 Sept. 1846.
37   *Sheffield and Rotherham Independent*, 18 Dec. 1846.
38   Bernard Timothy to Steward & Kincaid, land agents, 31 Dec. 1846 (in private possession).
39   Denis Mahon to John Ross Mahon, 5 Dec. 1846 (NLI, PM papers, MS 10,102 (2)).
40   Annotated notes included in the Strokestown estate rental, 1846 (SPHA).

Chapter 3: 'Destitution Prevails on this Country': Changing Attitudes on the Mahon Estate

1   Major Denis Mahon, to Relief Commissioners, Dublin Castle, 6 Aug. 1846 (NAI, RLFC 3/1/5166).
2   Denis Mahon to John Ross Mahon, 4 Mar. 1847 (NLI, PM papers, MS 10, 102 (3)). See also Thomas Boland to Thomas Roberts, 28 Dec. 1847 (SPHA).
3   Thomas Conry to Sir Richard Pennefather, 8 May 1846 (NAI, Outrage papers, Roscommon, 1846, 11349).
4   Quoted in *Hereford Journal*, 16 Dec. 1846.
5   See, for example, *RJ*, 7 March & 6 June 1846. It is interesting to note that he was also critical of the practice of wakes.
6   See, for example, *Leinster Express*, 18 Apr. 1846. A man named Maughan was severely beaten near Boyle for providing a cart for the army. Most people were afraid to report such outrages owing to the fear instilled by the Molly Maguires. Indeed, in 1849 a man arrested in Liverpool in connection with the murder of the Revd Lloyd, near Strokestown two years previous, claimed to have committed the crime because if he did not do it he would have been shot by the secret societies. See *Daily News*, 15 Feb. 1849.
7   Ibid., 1 July 1848. Increasingly, those convicted of crime were sentenced to transportation.
8   *RJ*, 7 Nov. 1846.
9   Ibid., 7 Jan. 1847.
10 See Charles E. Orser, 'An archaeology of a Famine-era eviction', *New Hibernia Review/Iris Éireannach Nua*, 9:1 (Spring, 2005), p. 45.
11 House of Lords, *Lands of Ballykilcline, County Roscommon. Returns of orders of the House of Lords, dated 16th and 19th February 1847* (London, 1847). See also Orser, 'An archaeology of a Famine-era eviction', pp 45–58.
12 Oliver McDonagh, 'Irish overseas emigration during the Famine' in Edward and Williams (eds), *The Great Famine: studies in Irish history* (Dublin, 1952), p. 337.
13 George Knox to John Burke, 24 May 1846 (NAI, Quit Rent papers, Roscommon, 1846). For accounts of the Ballykilcline estate see Robert Scally, *The end of hidden Ireland: rebellion, famine, and emigration* (Oxford, 1995) and Mary Lee Dunn, *Ballykilcline rising: from famine Ireland to immigrant America* (Amherst, MA, 2008).
14 See petition of Luke Cox of Strokestown, n.d. [1847] (NAI, Outrage papers, Roscommon 1847, 25/666).
15 Thomas Blakeney, Sub-Inspector to John Cusack, 15 July 1846 (in private possession).

16 House of Lords, *Lands of Ballykilcline*, p. 65. See also *London Standard*, 15 Jan. 1846.
17 Letter to the Officer Commanding, Athlone, 20 May 1847 (NAI, Outrage papers, Roscommon 1847).
18 Quoted in Mary Lee Dunn, 'Emigration from Ballykilcline' in *The Bonfire*, 3:2 (2001), pp 8–15.
19 Orser, 'An archaeology of a Famine-era eviction', p. 52.
20 Between 1998 and 2003, archaeologists working with Charles Orser discovered items that had been left behind by the Nary family, one of the evicted families, and were thus able to piece together their last weeks in Famine Ireland.
21 For more on these evictions see Crehan, *Marcella Gerrard*.
22 See Ciarán Reilly, *The Irish land agent, 1830–60: the case of King's County* (Dublin, 2014), p. 121.
23 There is evidence that George Knox was also acting as agent prior to the arrival of Guinness & Mahon. See Knox to Thomas Roberts, 24 Jan. 1848 (SPHA).
24 'Bond from John Ross Mahon and Robert Rundell Guinness of South Frederick Street in the city of Dublin who promised to pay Denis Mahon of Strokestown House in County Roscommon the sum of £5000, 27 Oct. 1846'; 'Bond from Sir James Mahon of Castlegar, County Galway and John Ross Mahon of South Frederick Street in the city of Dublin, to Denis Mahon of Strokestown House in County Roscommon of the sum of £2000, 27 Oct. 1846' (NLI, PM papers, MS 48,355 /16).
25 *Report from the Commissioners of Inquiry into the working of the Landlord and Tenant (Ireland) Act, and the acts amending same*, Parliamentary Papers, HC, 1881, xciii, p. 655.
26 John Ross Mahon to Denis Mahon, 28 Mar. 1847 (NLI, PM papers, MS 10,102 (2)).
27 'Memorandum on the management of the Strokestown estate by John Ross Mahon in his first year as agent for the late Major Mahon, Nov. 8, 1847' (NLI, PM papers, n. 558, p. 928).
28 Major Mahon to John Ross Mahon, 5 Jan. 1847 (NLI, PM papers, MS 10,102 (4)).
29 John Ross Mahon to Denis Mahon, 28 Feb. 1847 (NLI, PM papers, MS 10,102 (2)).
30 Major Denis Mahon to John Ross Mahon, 21 Nov. 1846 (NLI, PM papers, MS 10,102 (1)).
31 John Ross Mahon to Robert Guinness, 28 Nov. 1846 (NLI, PM papers, MS 10,102 (2)).
32 Denis Mahon to John Ross Mahon, 7 June 1847 (NLI, PM papers, MS 10, 102 (3)).
33 'Census recorded on Major Mahon's estate by the Strokestown Rental Office, recording townlands, parish, families, and number of persons or individuals, 21 Mar. 1847' (SPHA).
34 Major Denis Mahon to John Ross Mahon, 21 Nov. 1846 (NLI, PM papers, MS 10,102 (1)).
35 John Ross Mahon to Denis Mahon, 28 Feb. 1847 (NLI, PM papers, MS 10,102 (2)).
36 Ibid.
37 For example, Ross Mahon singled out the townland of Kilmacknany which consisted of 307 acres as being suitable for grazing.
38 Major Denis Mahon to John Ross Mahon, 14 Apr. 1847 (NLI, PM papers, MS 10,102 (1)).
39 See, for example, *Manchester Courier*, 29 May 184. See also 'Memorandum on the management' (NLI, PM papers, n. 558, p. 928).

Chapter 4: 'Orphaned to the World': Assisted Emigration in Practice

1 Major Denis Mahon to John Ross Mahon, 11 June 1847 (NLI, PM papers, MS 10,102 (1)).
2 'Major Mahon's memorandum of arrangements with tenants 30 Mar. – 6 Apr. 1847, no. 2' (SPHA).
3 Mick Heydon of North Yard was 74 years of age and had three sons in Newcastle-upon-Tyne, England. He was given assistance presumably because he had paid his rent in November 1844 when people held out against it.
4 'Major Denis Mahon's emigration account 1847' (NLI, PM papers, MS 10,138).
5 Major Denis Mahon to John Ross Mahon, 14 Sept. 1847 (NLI, PM papers, MS 10,102 (1)).
6 'Major Denis Mahon's emigration account 1847' (NLI, PM papers, MS 10,138).
7 These names are now commemorated on the Memorial Wall in Strokestown Park House, unveiled in May 2014.

8   The social memory of the scheme is particularly interesting. For example, Leo Tye, grandson of Daniel Tighe, orphaned at Grosse Île in 1847, claimed that the Queen of England had paid for the family's passage, suggesting that Britain was to blame for the Great Famine and ultimately their plight. See Marianna O'Gallagher, 'The orphans of Grosse Île: Canada and the adoption of Famine orphans, 1847-8' in Patrick O'Sullivan (ed.), *The meaning of Famine*, 6 vols (London, 2000), pp 90–1.
9   See, for example, *Manchester Courier*, 29 May 1847.
10 *RJ*, 3 July 1847. Ironically, the *Roscommon Journal*, particularly vociferous about the Mahon evictions, printed the Civil Bills and ejectment decrees that evicted tenants were presented with, making a handsome income in the bargain.
11 See, for example, P.J. Meghan, 'Stephen de Vere's voyage to Canada, 1847' in Etienne Rynne (ed.), *North Munster Studies: essays in commemoration of Monsignor Michael Moloney* (Limerick, 1967), pp 342–51. See also Donald McKay, *Flight from famine: the coming of the Irish to Canada* (Toronto, 1990), p. 287.
12 See Marianna O'Gallagher & Rose Masson Dompierre, *Eyewitness: Grosse Île 1847* (Quebec, 1995).
13 Another group of tenants from the townland of Castlenode were also selected for emigration, but Major Mahon feared that they would not be ready in time to be at Liverpool and aborted the plans for this journey.
14 For the arrival of the ships see Andre Charbonneau and Andre Sevigny, *1847 Grosse Île: a record of daily events* (Quebec, 1997).
15 *Toronto Globe*, 4 Aug. 1847.
16 Ibid.
17 Quoted in Edward Laxton, *The Famine ships: Irish exodus to America, 1846–51* (New York, 1998), p. 45.
18 *Quebec Morning Chronicle*, 19 July 1847.
19 *Toronto Globe*, 4 Aug. 1847.
20 *Quebec Morning Chronicle*, 19 July 1847.
21 Quoted in Marianna O'Gallagher, *The orphans of Grosse Île: gateway to Canada, 1832–1937* (Quebec, 1984), pp 90–1. Upon arrival in Canada, the Tighes, Daniel and Catherine, subsequently were recorded as Tye.
22 *The Morning Chronicle* (Québec), 9 Sept. 1847.
23 Ibid., pp 117–43.
24 Ibid. Both children were adopted by John Flanagan of Stoneham.
25 In 2013, Richard and Louisette Tye, descendants of Daniel and Catherine Tighe, returned to Strokestown for the Gathering.
26 O'Gallagher, *The orphans of Grosse Île*, pp 90–1.
27 Historian Michael Quigley believes that this figure could be almost double. See J.A. Jordan, *The Grosse Île tragedy and the monument to the Irish Famine victims, 1847* (Quebec, 1909), p. 12.
28 Darby Green was also given money to go; John Lyon surrendered two houses and plots before going to America at his own cost. A number of tenants were compensated because they were too old to travel. These included Pat Farrell, John Maguire and Bryan Hanahoe of Kilmacknary. See a variety of compensation files in the SPHA.
29 Thomas O'Farrell, Ballinafad to Henry Sandford Pakenham Mahon, 25 Mar. 1849 (SPHA).

Chapter 5: Targeting the 'Snug' Tenantry: Prelude to Murder

1 *The Tablet*, 27 Mar. 1847.
2 There were also huge division among the inhabitants of Strokestown owing to the general election of 1847, when it was claimed that priest and landlord battled for supremacy. About this election, Denis Mahon remarked that it was conducted 'messily' in Roscommon; a case simply of 'priest v bishop, priest v priest, landlord v tenant'. Major Denis Mahon to John Ross Mahon, 10 Aug. 1847 (NLI, PM papers, MS 10,102 (1)).
3 *The Examiner*, 13 Nov. 1847.

4 Other high-profile assassinations in nineteenth-century Ireland included: in 1839, Hector John Toler, 2nd earl of Norbury, who was murdered by tenants at Durrow, King's County; William Sydney Clements, 3rd earl of Leitrim, murdered in Donegal in 1878 by his tenants, and Lord Frederick Cavendish and Thomas Henry Burke, murdered in the Phoenix Park, Dublin, in May 1882. See, for example, Ciarán Reilly, 'Clearing the estate to fill the workhouse: King's County land agents and the Irish Poor Law Act of 1838' in Virginia Crossman and Peter Gray (eds), *Poverty and welfare in Ireland, 1838–1948* (Dublin, 2011), pp 145–62; A.P.W. Malcomson, *Virtues of a wicked earl: the life and legend of William Sydney Clements, 3rd earl of Leitrim, 1806–78* (Dublin, 2008); Senan Molony, *The Phoenix Park murders: conspiracy, betrayal and retribution* (Dublin, 2006).
5 Denis Mahon to John Ross Mahon, 10 June 1847 (NLI, PM papers, 10,102 (4)).
6 Major Denis Mahon to John Ross Mahon, 20 Oct. 1847 (NLI, PM papers, MS 10,102 (1)).
7 Major Denis Mahon to John Ross Mahon, 14 Sept. 1847 (NLI, PM papers, MS 10,102 (1)).
8 Major Denis Mahon to John Robinson, 14 June 1847 (NLI, PM papers, MS 10,102 (1)).
9 John Ross Mahon to HSP Mahon, 18 Feb. 1848 (SPHA).
10 Major Denis Mahon to John Ross Mahon, 11 June 1847 (NLI, PM papers, MS 10,102 (1)).
11 Major Denis Mahon to John Ross Mahon, 21 Sept. 1847 (NLI, PM papers, 10,102 (1)).
12 Major Denis Mahon to John Ross Mahon, 10 June 1847 (NLI, PM papers, MS 10,102 (1)).
13 *Bradford Observer*, 15 July 1847.
14 John Ross Mahon to Denis Mahon, 23 July 1847 (SPHA).
15 Major Denis Mahon to John Ross Mahon, 12 Aug. 1847 (NLI, PM papers, MS 10,102 (1)).
16 Major Denis Mahon to John Ross Mahon, 20 Oct. 1847 (NLI, PM papers MS 10,102 (1)).
17 See, for example, John Browne to John Ross Mahon, 17 Jan. 1847 (SPHA).
18 For an insight into the disputed nature of the location of the murder see Desmond Norton, 'Where was Denis Mahon shot', UCD Centre for Economic Research Working Paper Series; WP01/21 (Sept. 2001). Since the murder there has been debate as to where the incident actually happened and a number of locations cited. Determining the precise location is not helped by the fact that in the intervening period the landscape, mainly field divisions and boundaries, has changed significantly. It is my belief, however, that the murder took place in the townland of Dooherty. The targeting of this townland in the months after Mahon's death would support this theory.
19 'An Account of the probable expenditure required for keeping the house for Lord Hartland yearly including horses, carriages etc (c.1840)' (SPHA).
20 See, for example, Denis Mahon, 11 William St, Knightsbridge, London to Tom Conry, Strokestown, 11 Jan. 1844 (SPHA).
21 George White West, Ardinode House, Ballymore Eustace, Kildare to Thomas Roberts, 14 Aug. 1848 (SPHA).
22 Henry Sandford Pakenham Mahon to Thomas Roberts, 29 July 1848 (SPHA). Somewhat ironically, house recipes also included instructions on the making of potato cakes and fritters. See Various recipes, n.d. (NLI, PM papers, MS 10, 104).
23 In early 1852, for example, Thomas Roberts, the under-agent, was reminded to have the repairs to the roof and painting of the house 'done without delay ... a nice limestone colour ... not too dark so that the body of the house may match the wings'. See John Ross Mahon to Thomas Roberts, 12 Feb. & 6 Apr. 1852 (SPHA).
24 *FJ*, 20 Sept. 1848.
25 Revd Henry Brennan, PP of Kilglass to Henry Sandford Pakenham Mahon, 21 Dec. 1848 (SPHA).
26 Major Denis Mahon lamented that 'the election goes on messily. Priest v bishop, priest v priest, landlord v tenant'. See Major Denis Mahon to John Ross Mahon, 10 Aug. 1847 (NLI, PM papers, MS 10,102 (1)).
27 Quoted in Raymond Browne, *The destitution survey: reflections on the Famine in the diocese of Elphin* (Boyle, 1997), p. 75.
28 *The Tablet*, 27 Mar. 1847.
29 See, for example, 'Petition of the Kilbeg tenants, Feb. 1848' (SPHA).

30 'Marriage settlement made in 1847 on the intermarriage of Henry S. Pakenham (son of the Honorable and Reverend Henry Pakenham, Dean of St Patrick's and Christchurch Cathedral, Dublin) to Grace Catherine Mahon, daughter of Denis and Henrietta Mahon of Strokestown House, County Roscommon, 10 Mar. 1847' (NLI, PM papers, MS 48,355 /63). See also *FJ*, 17 Mar. 1847.

31 Supplementary report on the Pakenham-Mahon papers (from 1703), now in the National Library of Ireland, relating to lands in Co. Roscommon (National Library Report on Private Collections, No. 280). John Ainsworth's report on the Pakenham Mahon papers mentions Grace Mahon's 1847 diary, although no trace can now be found of this.

Chapter 6: 'Worse than Cromwell and Yet He Lives': the Murder of Major Mahon

1 *Roscommon and Leitrim Gazette*, 13 Nov. 1847.
2 *RJ*, 8 July 1847.
3 Major Denis Mahon to Revd Michael McDermott, 8 Sept. 1847 (SPHA).
4 Revd Michael McDermott to Major Denis Mahon, 9 Sept. 1847 (SPHA).
5 While the exchange of words between the pair has been disputed, Dr Terence Shanley testified to being present. See Dr Terence Shanley to Henry Sanford Pakenham Mahon, 2 May 1848 (SPHA).
6 *Hansard Parliamentary Debates*, vol. 95, series 3, 6 Dec. 1847, 680–81.
7 Ibid.
8 'Petition of Michael McDermott PP of Strokestown & Archdeacon of Elphin, John McDermott CC of Strokestown and James O'Reilly CC of Strokestown to the Lord Lieutenant', 25 Sept. 1846 (NAI, RLFC 3/2/25/58).
9 Connor had come to the attention of the police in Roscommon as early as 1840 when he was convicted of being part of a Ribbon conspiracy in Ballinamore, county Leitrim. Some accounts state that Connor was the leader of the Molly Maguires. See *Roscommon Leitrim Gazette*, 13 June & 18 July 1840.
10 Quoted in Browne (ed.), *The destitution survey*, p. 25.
11 These included James Farrell who died of 'congestive apoplexy' in Roscommon gaol. See T.F. Heath to Inspector General, 12 Nov. 1847 (NAI, Outrage papers, Roscommon, 1847, 25/709).
12 Martin Carrick to Thomas Blackeney, 26 Nov. 1847 (NAI, Outrage papers, Roscommon, 1848).
13 'Information of Thomas Tiernan relative to the murder of Major Mahon (NAI, Outrage papers, Roscommon, 1848).
14 An account of the clerk, Charles Costello by Dr Shanley, 9 May 1848 (SPHA).
15 *The Hull Packet and East Riding Times*, 23 Feb. 1849.
16 Martin Carrick to W. Miller, Inspector General, 13 Nov. 1847 (NAI, Outrage papers, Roscommon, 1848, 25/723).
17 John Ross Mahon to Henry Sandford Pakenham Mahon, 12 August 1848 (NLI, G&ML 32,023 (338)).
18 John Ross Mahon to Henry Sandford Pakenham Mahon, 29 Feb. 1848 (SPHA).
19 'List of Crown witnesses relating to the murder of Major Mahon' (NAI, Outrage papers, Roscommon, 1849, 25/358). See Mrs Mahon to Henry Sanford Pakenham Mahon, 27 Jan. 1848 (SPHA).
20 Copy of a letter to Michael Gardner, 23 Mar. 1849 (SPHA).
21 As late as May 1848 information regarding the murder of Major Mahon continued to pour into Strokestown House. See John Ross Mahon to Henry Sandford Pakenham Mahon, 30 May 1848 (NLI, PM papers, MS 10,103 (3)).
22 *Morning Chronicle*, 6 Nov. 1847.
23 *The Bathurst Advocate*, 1 Apr. 1848.
24 See, for example, coverage of the Mahon murder in *Sydney Chronicle*, 10 June 1848 and *Sydney Morning Herald*, 22 Feb. 1848.
25 Quoted in Kerr, *A nation of beggars*, p. 93.
26 Diary of Queen Victoria, 5 Nov. 1847 (Royal Archives, VIC/QUI/1847).

27 Prince Albert memorandum, 3 Dec. 1847 (Royal Archives, AD, 16/22).
28 Quoted in James Murphy, *Abject loyalty: nationalism and monarchy in Ireland during the reign of Queen Victoria* (Cork, 2001), p. 66.
29 Quoted in Robin Haines, *Charles Trevelyan and the Great Irish Famine* (Dublin, 2004), p. 381.
30 *Cork Examiner*, 3 Nov. 1847.
31 *Hansard*, xcv, 6 Dec. 1847, pp 675–84.
32 Ibid.
33 House of Commons Debate, 23 Nov. 1847, vol. 95, cc64–148.
34 *Times*, 1 Dec. 1847.
35 Quoted in Duffy, *The killing of Major Denis Mahon*, p. 168.
36 See, for example, *RJ*, 15 July 1848.
37 Quoted in Donnelly, *The Great Potato Famine*, p. 27.
38 *FJ*, 29 Aug. 1849.
39 *Times*, 23 Feb. 1848.
40 *FJ*, 29 Apr. 1848.
41 John Ross Mahon to Henry Sandford Pakenham Mahon, 29 Apr. 1848 (SPHA). A newspaper clipping in the Strokestown Park archive in Ross Mahon's hand notes how the bishop was in Cloonfad a few days before the evictions were issued and so meeting with his father and brother must have known what was to happen. See 'Various press clippings with annotations in the hand of John Ross Mahon' (SPHA).
42 *FJ*, 5 Jan. 1848.
43 *Evening Freeman*, 9 Dec. 1847.
44 Denis Kelly to Henry Sandford Pakenham Mahon, 11 June 1848 (SPHA).
45 John Ross Mahon to Marcus McCausland, 8 Dec. 1847 (NLI, Guinness & Mahon [G & M] Letter books, MS 32,019 (602–3)).
46 John Ross Mahon to Marcus McCausland, 18 Jan. 1848 (NLI, G&M Letter books, MS 32,019 (316–17)).
47 John Ross Mahon to Thomas Roberts, 20 Jan. 1848 (NLI, G&M Letter books, MS 32,019 (399)).
48 John Ross Mahon to Mrs Mahon, 24 June 1848 (NLI, G&M Letter books, MS 32,019 (433)). See also John Ross Mahon to Thomas Roberts, 7 Feb. 1848 (NLI, G&M Letter books, MS 32,019 (931)).
49 *The Times*, 9 Nov. 1847.
50 John Ross Mahon to Henry Sandford Pakenham Mahon, 4 Feb. 1848 (SPHA).
51 Henry Sandford Pakenham Mahon to Major Smyth, 68th Regiment, 3 Jan. 1848 (SPHA). The army frequently fell afoul of Pakenham Mahon for their behaviour: in January 1848 he instructed that 'soldiers are not to be in the demesne without an officer and are never to cross the grass; officers in the house should inform their servants about damage to the doors, walls etc.'
52 In 1777 Conolly McCausland, the younger, married Theodosia Mahon of Strokestown. Such was the encumbered nature of the McCausland property that a mortgage of £25,000 was taken out on his Roscommon estate between 1849 and 1855. McCausland had a protracted ejectment proceedings with a tenant Joseph Pins at Rairdeghra from 1843 to 1849. McCausland also took a protracted case against Major Denis Mahon in the wake of the 3rd Baron being declared a lunatic. By the mid-1850s part of the McCausland property in county Roscommon was sold in the Incumbered Estates Court, a fate that, by-and-large, escaped that of the Pakenham Mahon estate. By the mid-1850s Marcus McCausland put 2,000 acres of his Roscommon estates for sale in the Incumbered Estates Court for £44,825 or twenty-six years purchase. By the late 1840s there was confusion as to what townlands Marcus McCausland actually owned near Strokestown. See, for example, H. Hamilton to Henry Sandford Pakenham Mahon, 20 Apr. 1849 (SPHA).
53 Threatening letter sent to Henry Sandford Pakenham Mahon, n.d. (SPHA).
54 *Daily News*, 24 Nov. 1847.
55 *The Bristol Mercury*, 11 Dec. 1847. See also Thomas Roberts to John Ross Mahon, 12 Dec. 1848 (NLI, PM papers, MS 10, 103(1)).

56 Quoted in *Hull Packet and East Riding Times,* 12 Nov. 1847. In 1839 when Lady Hartland died her coffin was carried to the family vault by the tenants on the estate, as was the custom and tradition in rural Ireland. See *FJ*, 2 Jan. 1839.

Chapter 7: 'With Renewed Vigour': the Clearances Continued

1   *FJ*, 31 May 1849.
2   See, for example, John Murray to John Ross Mahon, 17 Dec. 1849 (SPHA).
3   John Ross Mahon to Henry Sanford Pakenham Mahon, 16 Dec. 1848 (NLI, MS 10,103 (1)).
4   See John Mahon to Thomas Roberts, 20 Nov. 1849 & William J. Peyton to Thomas Roberts, 18 May 1850 (SPHA).
5   Henry Sandford Pakenham Mahon to John Ross Mahon, 11 Jan. 1848 (NLI, PM papers, MS 10,103 (3)).
6   John Ross Mahon to Henry Sandford Pakenham Mahon, 10 Aug. 1848 (NLI, GML 32,023 (316–18)).
7   Ibid., 11 Jan. 1848 (NLI, PM papers, MS 10,103 (3)).
8   John Ross Mahon to Henry Sandford Pakenham Mahon, 20 Jan. 1848 (NLI, PM papers, MS 10,103 (3)).
9   Ibid., 13 Jan. 1848.
10 'List of persons in the following townlands from whom possession was taken on the 20, 21, 23 September 1848 and handed over to me on the part of the proprietor Henry Sandford Pakenham Mahon' (SPHA). Interestingly, a tenant at Dooherty, John McManaman, was reported to have given information relative to the murder, thus breaking with the societal norm of closing ranks.
11 John Ross Mahon to Henry Sandford Pakenham Mahon, 12 Aug. 1848 (NLI, GML 32,023 (338)).
12 J.R. Mahon to H.S.P. Mahon, 16 Oct. 1848 (SPHA).
13 John Ross Mahon to Henry Sandford Pakenham Mahon, 19 May 1848 (NLI, PM papers, MS 10,103 (3)). This was something that greatly troubled Ross Mahon: 'I am sorry that you cannot proceed further in giving gratuities to persons surrendering' he wrote to his employer, 30 May 1848 (ibid.).
14 Throughout 1848 there were active efforts to lease Strokestown Park House; for example, a Mr Fetherstone of county Wicklow looked to be given a twenty-one year lease but this along with other offers was declined (SPHA).
15 See, for example, William Lloyd to Henry Sandford Pakenham Mahon, 20 May 1850 (SPHA).
16 Martin Kelly to Thomas Roberts, 8 Dec. 1852 (SPHA).
17 Roger Murray to John Ross Mahon, 10 Nov. 1847 (SPHA).
18 *Illustrated London News*, 26 Aug. 1848.
19 See Christine Kinealy, *This great calamity: the Irish Famine, 1845–52* (Dublin, 1994), p. 218. See also *FJ*, 25 Sept. 1851.
20 *RJ*, 8 Jan. 1848.
21 Martin Kelly to Henry Sandford Pakenham Mahon, 9 Dec. 1851 (SPHA).
22 Michael Murray to Thomas Roberts, 19 Apr. 1850 (SPHA).
23 Thomas Roberts to Henry Sandford Pakenham Mahon, July 1849 (SPHA).
24 George Walpole to Thomas Roberts, 19 Mar. 1853 (SPHA).
25 John Ross Mahon to Henry Sandford Pakenham Mahon, 3 Aug. 1848 (NLI, PM papers, MS 10, 159).
26 Ibid.
27 George Knox, Clonfree House, to Bartholomew Mahon, 24 May 1849 (SPHA).
28 George Knox to Thomas Roberts, 8 June 1849 (SPHA). For an insight into the travails of middlemen see Ciarán Reilly, 'A middleman in the 1840s: Charles Carey and the Leinster Estate' in Patrick Cosgrove, Karol Mullaney-Dignam & Terence Dooley (eds), *The rise and fall of an Irish aristocratic family: the FitzGeralds of Kildare* (Dublin, 2014), pp 178–87.
29 Guinness & Mahon to Thomas Roberts, 17 Feb. 1851 (SPHA).
30 Distress notice issued on the lands of Revd Morton, Castlecoote, Dec. 1848 (SPHA).
31 This author is currently exploring the issue of culpability during the Great Irish Famine using Strokestown as a case study.

32 *RJ*, 13 Jan. 1849.
33 *FJ*, 18 Jan. 1849.
34 Anonymous (Strokestown shopkeeper) to Henry Sandford Pakenham Mahon, 1849 (SPHA).
35 See, for example, 'Names of tenants that have burned land on the Clien [sic] estate in the year 1851' (SPHA).
36 Thomas Conry to Thomas Roberts, 20 Apr. 1854 (SPHA). See also John Boyd to Thomas Roberts, 2 June 1851 (SPHA).
37 John Bruen, Cleen to Thomas Roberts, 23 Jan. 1850 (SPHA).
38 See, for example, Michael Murray to Thomas Roberts, 13 Dec. 1850 (SPHA).
39 John Hamilton to Thomas Roberts, 22 July 1852 (SPHA).
40 'Tenants who received Compensation for Surrender, 1848–49' (NLI, PM papers, MS 10, 159). See also John Robinson to Thomas Roberts, 13 Aug. 1849 (SPHA).
41 Head Constable of Drumsna Police to Thomas Roberts, n.d. (SPHA).
42 John Ross Mahon to Thomas Roberts, 3 May 1851 (SPHA).
43 Threatening letter sent to John Robinson, bailiff on the Strokestown estate, 5 Feb. 1848 (SPHA).
44 Michael Madden to Thomas Roberts, 1 June 1849 (SPHA).
45 Enclosed in a letter from George Walpole to Thomas Roberts, 18 June 1851 (SPHA).
46 Richard Cowen to Thomas Roberts, 8 July 1852. See also Thomas Roberts to John Ross Mahon, 8 July 1852 (SPHA).
47 Edward Giverin to Thomas Roberts, 25 Apr. 1850 (SPHA).
48 Guinness & Mahon to Thomas Roberts, 14 Apr. 1852 (SPHA). Others simply committed crimes to be transported or sent to prison. In 1850, John Cusack, a bailiff, informed Roberts that 'from what you told me of Casey he had no goods and that the best course would be to have him arrested'. See John Cusack to Thomas Roberts, 12 Jan. 1850 (SPHA).
49 Thomas O'Farrell to Henry Sandford Pakenham Mahon, 25 Mar. 1849 (SPHA).
50 Petition of Widow Cox, Scramogue, n.d. (NLI, PM papers, MS 10,101 (5)).
51 Pat Wallace to John Ross Mahon, 7 Aug. 1847 (SPHA).
52 Petition of Widow Bourke to John Ross Mahon, 1849 (SPHA).
53 Petition of the Widow Dignam of Curries, 30 Nov. 1849 (SPHA).
54 John & Catherine Maguire, Strokestown to Thomas Roberts, 11 Dec. 1849 (SPHA).
55 Petition of Widow Catherside to Thomas Roberts, 30 Nov. 1849 (SPHA).
56 Michael Farrell to John Ross Mahon, 15 Jan. 1848 (SPHA).
57 Poem of Patrick Kilmartin, Roscommon, 1851 (SPHA).
58 Petition of Ballinafad tenants to Revd Pakenham, 4 Nov. 1848 (SPHA).
59 *John O' Groat Journal*, 22 Aug. 1851.
60 Revd Joseph Egan to Thomas Roberts, 9 June 1858 (SPHA).
61 John Bruen to Thomas Roberts, 29 May 1851 (SPHA).
62 Thomas Roberts to Guinness & Mahon, 6 Feb. 1850 (SPHA).
63 Guinness & Mahon to Thomas Roberts, 1 July 1851 (SPHA).
64 Henry Sandford Pakenham Mahon to Thomas Roberts, 19 Nov. 1855 (SPHA).
65 John Ross Mahon to Thomas Roberts, 31 Mar. 1855 (SPHA).
66 Ibid., 28 Jan. 1859 (SPHA).
67 Ibid., 17 Mar. 1859 (SPHA).

Chapter 8: The Exodus Continues

1 *Hereford Journal*, 11 Feb. 1850.
2 See, for example, Thomas Roberts to Guinness & Mahon, 31 July 1852 (SPHA). See also *FJ*, 12 Aug. 1851.
3 *FJ*, 24 Aug. 1852.
4 Hugh J. Flynn to Thomas Roberts, 21 Sept. 1853 (SPHA).

5   *FJ*, 3 Sept. 1852.
6   For an insight into the crimes committed in Strokestown during this period see the Roscommon Outrage papers in the NAI
7   *Ipswich Journal*, 25 Jan. 1851.
8   See 'Petition of the Kilbeg tenants', Feb. 1848 (SPHA). There is evidence that some left in small groups. For example, Strokestown natives Mary Carney, Thomas Keely, Elizabeth McAlany, John Moran, Mary Morvey and Fanny and Susan Rutherford were on board the ship *Sheridan*, which arrived in New York on 15 Dec. 1848.
9   Alex Ballintine to Thomas Roberts, 27 Apr. 1850 (SPHA).
10   John Rush to John Ross Mahon, 1 Jan. 1848 (SPHA).
11   Henry Sandford Pakenham Mahon to Thomas Roberts, 23 Dec. 1847 (SPHA).
12   Major Denis Mahon to Tom Conry, 10 July 1846 (NLI, PM papers, MS 10,101 (5)).
13   *RJ*, 1 July 1848.
14   John Killurin to Thomas Roberts, 18 Dec. 1848 (SPHA).
15   *Inverness Courier*, 11 July 1850.
16   William Flood to Thomas Roberts, 5 Apr. 1852 (SPHA).
17   See Guinness & Mahon to John Ross Mahon, 19 Mar. 1852 (SPHA).
18   Guinness & Mahon to Thomas Roberts, 19 Mar. 1852 (SPHA)
19   Archibald McIntyre, St Patrick's Head, Van Dieman's Land, on behalf of Patrick Mally, to Edmund Carr, Kilbride parish, Co. Roscommon, 9 Mar. 1847 (PRONI, T/3650/9). See also Henry Sandford Pakenham Mahon to Thomas Roberts, 7 Jan. 1860 (SPHA).
20   See Guinness & Mahon to Thomas Roberts, 6 Apr. 1852 & 12 Mar. 1853 (SPHA).
21   For an in-depth insight into the fate of many Irish emigrants in the nineteenth century see Regina Donlon, 'Go west and grow up with the country: a study of German and Irish immigrant communities in the American Midwest, 1850–1900' (PhD, NUI Maynooth, 2013).
22   Edward Martin, Tapscott's American Packet Office, 7 Eden Quay, Dublin to Guinness & Mahon, 10 Apr. 1855 (SPHA).
23   As late as 1857 tenants were still appealing to be assisted in emigration; in that year Mary Connor, a widow, appealed for assistance to America (SPHA)
24   Denis Sweeney to Thomas Roberts, 10 Aug. 1852 (SPHA).
25   'Precognition against Mary Wilson, Sarah McKendrick for the crime of theft, 1853' (National Records of Scotland, Crown Office precognitions, 1853, AD 14/53/61).
26   *South Side Signal*, 17 July 1875.
27   Mary Hester of Strokestown was another fever victim who was hospitalized in New Orleans. See the records of the Irish emigrants in the New Brunswick Almshouse at http://archives.gnb.ca/Irish/Databases/Almshouse/?culture=en-CA
28   J. Thomas Scharf, *History of Western Maryland: being a history of Frederick, Montgomery, Carroll, Washington, Allegany, and Garrett Counties from the earliest period to the present day; including biographical sketches of their representative men*, 2 vols (Philadelphia, 1882), ii, p. 1419.
29   See, for example, the exploits of James Beirne who opened his own boarding house for Irish emigrants. *Boston Pilot*, 3 Sept. 1856.
30   See Tyler Anbinder, 'Moving beyond "rags to riches": New York's Irish Famine immigrants and their surprising savings accounts', *Journal of American History*, 99 (Dec. 2012), pp 741–70. I am grateful to Mary Lee Dunn for bringing this to my attention. And what of the Ballykilcline natives who sailed in 1847 and 1848? In total 368 people sailed, leaving in five groups from Liverpool between September 1847 and the spring of 1848. Their story has been meticulously charted by Mary Lee Dunn in her book *Ballykilcline rising*, which includes details on the fate of the Padians, McGintys and Carlons among others. Today, the Ballykilcline Emigrant Society is perhaps one of the most vibrant groups of Famine-era descendants in America.
31   From 1831 to 1921 the *Boston Pilot* newspaper printed a 'Missing Friends' column with advertisements from

award of the Order of Menelik of Ethiopia. He later gained the rank of major in the service of the Grenadier Guards.
3 'Notes prepared for the coming-of-age speech of Nicholas Hales Pakenham Mahon, 1947' (SPHA).
4 *Aberdeen Evening Express*, 28 June 1883. Another misfortune, largely forgotten, befell Strokestown House in April 1851, when the son of Henry Grattan Curran, magistrate at Strokestown, was accidently shot in the bed chamber. It appears that Curran, the grandson of John Philpot Curran, was playing with a gun he thought was unloaded. The remains were consigned to the Mahon vault on the wishes of Mrs Mahon. See *Daily News*, 28 April 1851.
5 Quoted in Museum Panel, Irish National Famine Museum, Strokestown.
6 *Irish Times*, 3 Apr. 1962. The murder of Denis Mahon was also raised in the course of a Dáil Éireann debate in 1995 when Deputy John Connor, Longford–Roscommon TD, claimed that 'the Famine is etched in the consciousness of the people'. See Dáil Éireann, vol. 456, 5 Oct. 1995.
7 Evidence of Ide Ni Rian of Bridge Street, Strokestown, given to the Schools Manuscript Commission (Roscommon County Library).
8 'Statement of Patrick Mullooly, Kiltrustan, Strokestown, county Roscommon' (NAI, BOMH WS 1,087).
9 Scally, *The end of hidden Ireland*, p. 39. The murder has been the subject of numerous studies in recent years: both Patrick Vesey's *The murder of Major Mahon, Strokestown, county Roscommon, 1847* (Dublin, 2008) and Duffy's *The killing of Major Denis Mahon: a mystery of old Ireland* (Boston, 2007) examine the murder in a forensic manner, while Charles Orser, Anne Coleman, Robert Scally and Desmond Norton have all made reference to the murder in their own studies.
10 Likewise, there were several variations of the events which led to his murder, including the claim that the major's carriage and horse ran into Strokestown empty, signalling to the local community that the foul deed had been carried out.
11 Brodie and Brock Thoene, *All rivers to the sea: the Galway chronicles* (Nashville, 2001).
12 See Margaret Greenwood, Mark Connolly and Geoff Wallis, *Rough guide to Ireland* (London, 2003), p. 520; David Quinn, *It may be forever: an Irish rebel on the American frontier* (Indiana, 2005), p. 27.
13 Quoted on Exhibition Panel, Irish National Famine Museum, Strokestown Park House.
14 George Petrie, *The ancient music of Ireland* (Dublin, 1855), p. 55.
15 Quoted in Haines, *Charles Trevelyan*, p. 22.
16 William Carleton, *The Black Prophet: a tale of Irish Famine* (Dublin, 1847, repr., Shannon, 1972), pp 56–7.
17 Cormac Ó Gráda, *Ireland's Great Famine: interdisciplinary perspectives* (Dublin, 2006), p. 217.
18 Denis Kelly to Thomas Roberts, 3 June 1851 (SPHA).
19 Quoted in Cathal Pórtéir, *Famine echoes* (Dublin, 1995), p. 214. These were the class who had come through the Famine unscathed and had sufficient capital to purchase land. They included, for example, Thomas Dolan, a cart maker at Strokestown, who in 1853 had sufficient capital to buy land valued at over £2,000 in the Encumbered Estates Court. And individual wealth was evident in a number of other instances; for example, over forty people subscribed to a testimonial to Thomas Moore in 1852. See *FJ*, 11 May 1852 & 18 Feb. 1853
20 Anonymous letter to Thomas Roberts, 1851 (SPHA).
21 See George Browne to Thomas Roberts, 10 Mar. 1855 (SPHA).
22 Revd James Nally to Thomas Roberts, 14 Feb. 1851 (SPHA). In 1862 Revd William Brennan sought ten acres of land for his brother. See Revd William Brennan to Thomas Roberts, 9 Feb. 1862 (SPHA).
23 John Boyd to Thomas Roberts, 2 June 1851 (SPHA).
24 Helen O'Brien, *The Famine clearances in Toomevara, county Tipperary* (Dublin, 2010). See, for example, Hugh Croghan to John Ross Mahon, 21 July 1848 (SPHA).
25 Petition of widow Kilmartin to Thomas Roberts, 14 July 1848 (SPHA).
26 John Ross Mahon to Thomas Roberts, 14 Apr. 1852 (SPHA).
27 'Accounts of Lord Hartland mainly concerning house repairs 1833–49' (NLI, PM papers, MS 10,159).
28 David Nally, *Human incumbrances: political violence and the Great Irish Famine* (Notre Dame, IN, 2011).

29 See, for example, Pat Wallace to John Ross Mahon, 7 Aug. 1847 (SPHA).
30 Brendán MacSuibhne and David Dickson (eds), *The outer edge of Ulster: a memoir of social life in nineteenth-century Donegal* (Dublin, 2001), p. 230.
31 John McCann to Thomas Roberts, 22 May & 16 Oct. 1849 (SPHA).
32 John McCann to Thomas Roberts, 16 Oct. 1849 (SPHA).
33 John McCann to Thomas Roberts, 4 Sept. 1848. (SPHA).
34 Pat Gibbons to John Ross Mahon, 13 Dec. 1849 (SPHA).
35 See, for example, the petition of James Heeney to John Ross Mahon, 20 Feb. 1849 (SPHA).
36 Donnelly, *The Great Potato Famine*, p. 38.
37 Ibid., p. 199.
38 These attitudes mirrored sentiments elsewhere. At Edenderry in King's County, for example, in 1849 the Board of Guardians passed a resolution in an effort to avert crowds of paupers from Galway and other Famine stricken counties inundating the town. In order to do so they decided to transfer paupers found in the town to Dublin: 'The people of Edenderry are determined not to have the frightful scenes of other places enacted there, of hundreds of corpses lying unburied on the roads and ditches and devoured by dogs' it concluded. See *FJ*, 28 May 1849.
39 'Anonymous letter (from a shopkeeper) in Strokestown to Henry Sandford Pakenham Mahon, Oct. 1849' (SPHA).
40 John Ross Mahon to Henry Sanford Pakenham Mahon, 20 Jan. 1848 (SPHA).
41 The contrasting fortunes of the people of county Roscommon was aptly illustrated in the gross overcrowding and disease at the workhouse in Roscommon town at the close of 1849 (there were over 2,500 'inmates'), while the 'great fair' of Strokestown was well attended with fat cattle making the best prices. *FJ*, 15 Dec. 1849. Prior to the opening of the workhouse in Strokestown in 1852, the poor were temporarily relieved at Ardkeena, where an auxiliary workhouse was erected. Conditions there were said to have been appalling but proposals to teach industry by John Darcy, chairman of the Strokestown Union, highlighted that some efforts were being made to improve the lot of its inmates. See *FJ*, 6 Jan. 1849 & 28 Jan. 1852. See also *Dublin Builder*, 1 Aug. 1862.
42 'Roscommon Union Kilgaffin Electoral division: Return of paupers who were and are in the workhouse from 25th March last to the present date. Dated 17th November 1851. Compiled by W.J. Stanley, the late relieving officer' (SPHA).
43 John Robinson to Thomas Roberts, 13 Aug. 1849 (SPHA).
44 President Higgins' comments were made at the Overseas Great Irish Famine Commemoration in Boston in May 2012. Quoted in *Irish Times*, 8 May 2012.

Postscript: The Making of the Irish National Famine Museum

1 Ridgway, 'Making and meaning', p. 229.
2 President Mary Robinson, speaking at the launch of the Famine Museum, 15 May 1994. *Irish Times*, 16 May 1994.
3 *Irish Times*, 23 May 1988.
4 Ibid., 30 May 1992.
5 *New York Times*, 12 June 1994.
6 Dáil Éireann, vol. 440, 24 Mar. 1994: National Monuments (Amendment) Bill, 1993 [Seanad]: Second Stage.
7 *Cara*, July/August 1994.
8 *Irish Times*, 13 Oct. 1992.
9 *The Spectator*, 7 Aug. 1993.
10 *The Guardian*, 14 May 1994.
11 Quoted in Dooley, 'The Big House and Famine memory', p. 626.
12 *Roscommon Champion*, 20 May 1994.
13 *Sunday Times*, 8 May 1994. This was a point that Declan Jones concurred with, arguing that 'these original

documents [were put] on display so that people could get a greater awareness of the conditions that existed. Its purpose is a dual one – largely educational, making us more aware of our own history; but it also has the effect of balancing to an extent the history of the "Big House" in that it seeks to represent the lives of the particular tenants living on the estate.' See Lorraine Pearsall, 'Strokestown Park and the making of the Famine museum: an interview with Declan Jones', *South Carolina Review* (1999), p. 196.

14   *Town & Country*, Oct. 1993.
15   See, for example, Terry Eagleton, 'Feeding off history', *The Observer*, 20 Feb. 1994; Niall Ó Ciosáin, 'Hungry grass', *Circa*, 68 (Summer, 1994), p. 24 and Peter Gray, 'Strokestown Famine Museum', *History Ireland*, 2:2 (Summer, 1994), p. 5.
16   *The Tablet*, 21 May 1994.
17   Niamh Ann Kelly, 'Similarity and difference: the appearance of suffering at the Strokestown Famine Museum' in Annette Hoffman and Esther Peeran (eds), *Representation matters: (re)articulating collective identities in a post colonial world* (New York, 2010), p. 140.
18   Christi Daugherty and Jack Jewers, *Frommer's Ireland* (New Jersey, 2011), p. 55.
19   See Dooley, 'The Big House and Famine memory: Strokestown Park House' in Crowley et al. (eds), *Atlas of the Great Irish Famine*, p. 629.

Bibliography

PRIMARY SOURCES

I. Manuscript Material

National Archives of Ireland
Bureau of Military History Witness Statements; Outrage Papers; Relief Commission Papers; State of the Country Papers

National Library of Ireland
Guinness & Mahon Letter books; Mahon of Castlegar papers; Pakenham Mahon papers

National Records of Scotland
Crown Office precognitions papers

OPW/NUIM Archive & Research Centre
Strokestown Park House Archive

Public Records Office of Northern Ireland
Copy charge submitted by Denis Mahon, to the Committee of the estate of the lunatic, Lord Hartland, 25 Apr. 1845; Diary of Sir Alexander Crichton, 1829

Roscommon County Library
Roscommon Workhouse Minute Books; Strokestown Workhouse Minute Books; Schools Manuscript Commission

Royal Archives London
Diary of Queen Victoria; Prince Albert memorandum.

II. Newspapers

Aberdeen Evening Express; *Bath Chronicle and Weekly Gazette*; *Boston Pilot*; *Bristol Mercury*; *Carlisle Journal*; *Cassville Index*; *Cork Examiner*; *Daily News*; *Derby Mercury*; *Farmers' Gazette*; *Evening Freeman*; *Freeman's Journal*; *Hereford Journal*; *Ipswich Journal*; *Irish Independent*; *Irish Reporter*; *Irish Times*; *John O'Groat Journal*; *Kentish Gazette*; *King's County Chronicle*; *Leinster Express*; *Leitrim Observer*; *Liverpool Mercury*; *London Standard*; *Manchester Courier*; *Morning Chronicle*; *Norfolk News*; *Plymouth and Cornish Advertiser*; *Preston Chronicle*; *Quebec Chronicle*; *Roscommon Journal*; *Roscommon & Leitrim Gazette*; *Sheffield and Rotherham Independent*; *South Side Signal*; *Sunday Independent*; *Sydney Chronicle*; *Sydney Morning Herald*; *The Bathurst Advocate*; *The Examiner*; *The Hull Packet and East Riding Times*; *The Morning Chronicle* (Québec); *The Observer*; *The Tablet*; *Toronto Globe*

III. Contemporary Works

Carleton, William, *The Black Prophet : a tale of Irish famine* (Dublin, 1847, rep., Shannon, 1972)
Gibbon, Skeffington, *The recollections of Skeffington Gibbon from 1796 to the present year, 1829; being an epitome of*

the lives and characters of the nobility and gentry of Roscommon; the genealogy of those who are descended from the kings of Connaught; and a memoir of the late Madame O'Conor Don (Dublin, 1829)

House of Lords, *Lands of Ballykilcline, County Roscommon. Returns of orders of the House of Lords, dated 16th and 19th February 1847* (London, 1847)

Petrie, George, *The ancient music of Ireland* (Dublin, 1855)

Pigot's Directory (1824)

Scharf, J. Thomas, *History of Western Maryland: being a history of Frederick, Montgomery, Carroll, Washington, Allegany, and Garrett Counties from the earliest period to the present day; including biographical sketches of their representative men* (2 vols, Philadelphia, 1882)

Wakefield, Edward, *An account of Ireland, statistical and political* (2 vols, London, 1812)

Weld, Isaac, *Statistical survey of the county of Roscommon* (Dublin, 1832)

Young, Arthur, *A tour in Ireland: with general observations on the present state of the kingdom made in the years 1776, 1777 and 1778, and brought down to the end of 1779* (repr. Shannon, 1970)

IV. Parliamentary Publications

See *First report from His Majesty's commissioners for inquiring into the condition of the poorer classes in Ireland*, with appendix (A.) and supplement, 1835 (369)

Abstract of the police reports of some of the principal outrages in the counties Tipperary, Clare, Limerick, Leitrim and Roscommon in the year 1845, HC, 1846, 710

Report of Her Majesty's Commissioners of Inquiry into the working of the Landlord and Tenant (Ireland) Act, 1870, and the acts amending the same, 1881 [C.2779] [C.2779-I] [C.2779-II] [C.2779-III]

SECONDARY SOURCES

Anbinder, Tyler, 'Moving beyond "rags to riches": New York's Irish Famine immigrants and their surprising savings accounts', *Journal of American History*, 99 (Dec. 2012), pp 741–70

Bourke, P.M.A., 'The scientific investigation of the potato blight in 1845–6', *Irish Historical Studies*, 13:49 (1962), pp 26–32

Browne, Raymond, *The destitution survey: reflections on the Famine in the diocese of Elphin* (Boyle, 1997)

Charbonneau, Andre and Andre Sevigny, *1847 Grosse Île: a record of daily events* (Quebec, 1997)

Crehan, Tom, *Marcella Gerrard's Galway estate, 1820–70* (Dublin, 2013)

Donlon, Regina, 'Go west and grow up with the country: a study of German and Irish immigrant communities in the American Midwest, 1850–1900' (PhD, NUI Maynooth, 2013)

Donnelly, James, *The Great Irish potato Famine* (Stroud, 2001)

Dooley, Terence, 'The Big House and Famine memory' in John Crowley and William Smyth (eds), *Atlas of the Great Irish Famine* (Cork, 2012), pp 622–9

Doyle, Anthony, *Charles Powell Leslie II's estates at Glaslough, county Monaghan, 1800–1841* (Dublin, 2001)

Duffy, Peter, *The killing of Major Denis Mahon: a mystery of old Ireland* (New York, 2007)

Dunn, Mary Lee, *Ballykilcline rising: from Famine Ireland to immigrant America* (Amherst, MA, 2008)

—— 'Emigration from Ballykilcline', *The Bonfire*, 3:2 (2001), pp 8–15

Edwards, R.D., and T.D. Williams (eds), *The Great Famine: studies in Irish history, 1845–52* (Dublin, 1956)

Gray, Peter, 'Strokestown Famine Museum', *History Ireland*, 2:2 (Summer, 1994)

Greenwood, Margaret, Mark Connolly, and Geoff Wallis, *Rough guide to Ireland* (London, 2003)

Haines, Robin, *Charles Trevelyan and the Great Irish Famine* (Dublin, 2004)

Hood, Susan, 'The landlord-planned nexus at Strokestown, county Roscommon: a case study of an Irish estate town, c.1660–c.1925' (PhD, University of Ulster, 1994)

Huggins, Michael, *Social conflict in pre-Famine Ireland: the case of county Roscommon* (Dublin, 2004)

Irvine, Leigh H. (ed.), *History of the new California, its resources and people* (California, 1905)
Jordan, A., *The Grosse Île tragedy and the monument to the Irish Famine victims, 1847* (Quebec, 1909)
Kelly, Niamh Ann, 'Similarity and difference: the appearance of suffering at the Strokestown Famine Museum' in Annette Hoffman and Esther Peeran (eds), *Representation matters: (re)articulating collective identities in a post colonial world* (New York, 2010), pp 133–53
Kerr, Donal, *A nation of beggars: priests, people, and politics in Famine Ireland, 1846–1852* (Oxford, 1998)
Kinealy, Christine, *This great calamity: the Irish famine, 1845–52* (Dublin, 1994)
Laxton, Edward, *The Famine ships: Irish exodus to America, 1846–51* (New York, 1998)
Lennon, Mike, 'The history of Strokestown's houses – part 2', *County Roscommon Historical and Archaeological Journal*, 30 (2012), pp 64–6
Lyne, Gerard, *The Lansdowne estates in Kerry under the agency of W.S. Trench, 1849-72* (Dublin, 2001)
MacSuibhne, Brendán and David Dickson (eds), *The outer edge of Ulster: a memoir of social life in nineteenth-century Donegal* (Dublin, 2001)
McKay, Donald, *Flight from famine: the coming of the Irish to Canada* (Toronto, 1990)
Malcomson, A.P.W., *Calendar of the Rosse papers* (Dublin, 2007)
—— and Patrick Walsh, *Calendar of the Connolly papers* (Dublin, 2010)
Meghan, P.J., 'Stephen de Vere's voyage to Canada, 1847' in Etienne Rynne (ed.), *North Munster Studies: essays in commemoration of Monsignor Michael Moloney* (Limerick, 1967), pp 342–51
Murphy, James, *Abject loyalty: nationalism and monarchy in Ireland during the reign of Queen Victoria* (Cork, 2001)
Nally, David, *Human incumbrances: political violence and the Great Irish Famine* (Notre Dame, IN, 2011)
Norton, Desmond, 'Where was Denis Mahon shot', UCD Centre for Economic Research Working Paper Series; WP01/21 (Sept. 2001)
O'Brien, Helen, *The Famine clearance in Toomevara, county Tipperary* (Dublin, 2010)
Ó Ciosáin, Niall, 'Hungry grass', *Circa*, 68 (Summer, 1994), pp 24–7
O'Gallagher, Marianna, 'The orphans of Grosse Île: Canada and the adoption of Famine orphans, 1847–8' in Patrick O'Sullivan (ed.), *The meaning of Famine*, 6 vols (London, 2000), pp 81–111
—— *The orphans of Grosse Île: gateway to Canada, 1832–1937* (Quebec, 1984)
—— and Rose Masson Dompierre, *Eyewitness: Grosse Île 1847* (Quebec, 1995)
Ó Gráda, Cormac, *Ireland's Great Famine: interdisciplinary perspectives* (Dublin, 2006)
Orser, Charles E., 'An archaeology of a Famine-era eviction', *New Hibernia Review / Iris Éireannach Nua*, 9:1 (Spring, 2005), pp 176–92
Pearsall, Lorraine, 'Strokestown Park and the making of the Famine museum: an interview with Declan Jones', *South Carolina Review* (1999), pp 195–201
Pórtéir, Cathal, *Famine echoes* (Dublin, 1995)
Quinn, David, *It may be forever: an Irish rebel on the American frontier* (Indiana, 2005)
Reilly, Ciarán, *The Irish Land Agent, 1830–1860: the case of King's County* (Dublin, 2014)
—— 'A middleman in the 1840s: Charles Carey and the Leinster Estate' in Patrick Cosgrove, Karol Mullaney-Dignam & Terence Dooley (eds), *Aspects of Irish aristocratic life: essays on the FitzGerald's of Carton House* (Dublin, 2014), pp 178–86
—— *John Plunket Joly and the Great Famine in King's County* (Dublin, 2012)
—— 'Clearing the estate to fill the workhouse: King's County land agents and the Irish Poor Law Act of 1838' in Virginia Crossman and Peter Gray (eds), *Poverty and welfare in Ireland, 1838–1948* (Dublin, 2011), pp 145–62
Ridgway, Christopher, 'Making and meaning in the historic house' in Terence Dooley and Christopher Ridgway (eds), *The Irish country house: past, present and future* (Dublin, 2011), pp 203–43
Scally, Robert, *The end of hidden Ireland: rebellion, famine, and emigration* (Oxford, 1995)
Thoene, Brodie and Brock, *All rivers to the sea: the Galway chronicles* (Nashville, 2001)
Woods, C.J., *Travellers' accounts as source material for Irish historians* (Dublin, 2009)

Illustration Credits

Unless otherwise stated all images and archival material are courtesy of the Strokestown Park House Archive and the Irish National Famine Museum.

page 8 'Gothic Arch at Strokestown' & 'Lord Hartland's bookplate' (Liam Byrne); page 9 'Strokestown Park House' (Eunan Sweeney); page 13 'Map of the Mahon estate' (Fidelma Byrne); page 30 'The Conacre disturbances' (*Freeman's Journal*, 2 April 1845); page 48 'Paupers standing in line for Indian meal, 1847' (National Library of Ireland); page 51 'Meeting of the Strokestown tradesmen' (*Freeman's Journal*, 25 Sept. 1846); page 59 'Edward Murphy' (Margaret Garvey); page 61 'Queuing for Indian meal, 1847' (National Library of Ireland); page 68 'Emigrants arrival at Cork – A scene on the quay' (*Illustrated London News*, 10 May 1851); page 74 'The passage money paid' (*ILN*, 10 May 1851); page 76 'The embarkation at Waterloo Docks' (*Illustrated London News*); page 77 'Mary Tye' (Tye family); 'The ship fever in Canada' (*Liverpool Mercury*, 3 Sept. 1847); page 78 (*Illustrated London News*, 22 Dec. 1849); page 85 'Michael Calhoun Dufficy' (Mike Dufficy); page 87 'Drawing Room & Kitchen at Strokestown' (Eunan Sweeney); page 89 'The day after ejectment' (*Illustrated London News*, 16 Dec. 1849); page 92 'Report on the murder of Denis Mahon' (*Belfast Newsletter*, 5 Nov. 1847); page 99 'Standing in line for Indian meal, 1847' (National Library of Ireland); page 102 'Tradesmen defend Rev McDermott' (*Freeman's Journal*, 2 Jan. 1848); page 112 'The ejectment' (*Illustrated London News*, 16 Dec. 1849); page 132 'Edwin O'Beirne' (Dorothy Reed); page 134 'Matilda O'Beirne (Dorothy Reed); page 136 'Coggins family enter Strokestown workhouse' (*Freeman's Journal*, 3 Sept. 1850); 'Strokestown Workhouse minute book' (Roscommon County Library); page 139 Pat Hanly (Ciarán Reilly); page 143 (Barbara Scanlon); page 144 'Elijah Impey' (Dorothy Reed); page 150 'Strokestown Catholic Church' (Liam Byrne); page 154 'Edwin O'Beirne' (Dorothy Reed); page 168 'Extract from Strokestown Workhouse Minute Book' (Roscommon County Library).

Index

Page numbers in bold refer to illustrations

assisted emigration (*panel*), 72

Ballykilcline, 47, 51–3
Boggs, Thomas Wynne, 113
Boyd, Revd, 88–9
Brassington & Gale, land surveyors, 57
Brennan, Revd Henry, PP Kilglass, 88
Browne, Bishop George, 50, 104
Browne, Patrick, middleman, 51, 82–3, 104, 118, 155–6
Bruen, John, strong farmer, 123, **168**

Callery, Jim, 1, 76, 184, **185**
Carleton, William, 172
Carlos, Charles, process server, 175
Cassells (Castle), Richard, 18
Clare, county, 29
Clonbrock, Lord, 86
Cloonahee document, **2**
Coggins, Frank, emigrant, 136
Coleman, John, emigrant, 141
Connor, Andrew, ribbonman, 97–8
Connor, Martin, head gardener, 18
Conry, Thomas, land agent, 28, 42, 46, 118
Cooney, John, process server, 175
Costello, Charles, clerk, 98
Cox, Widow, tenant, 44
Crofton, Lord, 162

de Vere, Stephan, landlord, 68
Dillon, James, TD, 166
Dodd, Luke, former curator of Irish National Famine Museum, 182–4
Donnell, James, landscape gardener, 18
Donnelly, James Jr, historian, 176
Dooley, Terence, historian, 1, 9
Dorian, Hugh, 171
Douglas, Dr George, 71
Doyle, Martin, surveyor, 160
Dufficy, Martin Calhoun, 85, **85**

Erin's Queen, 71–3,
evictions and clearances (*panel*), 122

Farnham, Lord, 101

Gardiner, Michael, suspect in Mahon murder, 100
Gerrard, Marcella, 53–4
Grattan, Henry, 101
Gray, James, board of works engineer, 35
Gray, Peter, historian, 179–81
Grosse Ile, 71–6, 163
Guinness & Mahon, land agents, 137
Guinness, Robert Rundall, 54
Gurtoose, townland, **21**

Hales, Major Stuart, **182**
Hanly, Patrick, emigrant, **139**, 143
Hanly, Revd John, PP Kilgaffin, 172
Harrison, Christopher, land agent , 35
Herans, Andrew, land agent, 133
Higgins, Michael D., President of Ireland, 177, **185**, 187
Hood, Susan, historian, 14
Horan, Michael, land surveyor, 157

Impey, Elijah, emigrant, **144**, 154
Irish National Famine Museum, 76, 171, 179–87
Irish Poor Law Act (1838), 29
Irwin, Richard, Justice of the Peace, 30
Irwin, Valentine, land agent, 30

John Munn, 71–3
Jones, Declan, Westward Holdings, 181–2

Kelly, Denis, landlord, 106
Kelly, Pat, emigrant, **143**
Kenny, Enda, Taoiseach, **187**
Keogh, Peter, landlord, 117
Kilglass, 27
Kiltrustan, 88
Knox, George, Crown Agent, 33, 117–18

Lauder, Alonso, landlord, 133
Limerick, county, 29
Lloyd, Revd, Elphin, 109
Lorton, Lord, 86
Lynn, John, architect, 20

Mahon, John, 18
Mahon, John Ross, 38, **40**, 40, 54, 57, 59, 63, 66–7, 84, 95, 98, 107–8, 112, 117, 123, 125, 131, 147, 150, 160–1
Mahon, Major Denis, 15, 26
    dispute with Revd McDermott, 91–7
    arrival at Strokestown, 23–6
    assisted emigration scheme, 65–71
    murder of, and subsequent controversy, 98–107
Mahon, Maurice, Lord Hartland, **8**, 20
Mahon, Nicholas, 14, 17–18
Mahon, Revd Maurice, 3rd Baron Hartland, **14**, 14–15, 22–3, 33
Mahon, Theodosia, **16**
Mahon, Thomas, **12**, 18
Mahon, Thomas, 2nd Lord Hartland, 20–1
McAleese, Mary, former President of Ireland, ix–x, 3, 6, **185**
McCann, John, watcher, 176
McCausland family, 108
McCausland, Marcus, 16, 23
McDermott, Revd Michael, PP Strokestown, 29–30, 38, 79, 82, 91–4, 97, 102–3, 105, 150, 160
McLaughlin, Pat, land surveyor, 147
McManus, Liz, TD, 180
Michael Dufficy, 85
Molly Maguires, 50, 53, 125
Morton, Revd Joseph, 118, 152
Mulloolly, Patrick, 166
Murphy, Edward, Public Works Scheme engineer, **59**
Myers, Kevin, journalist, 180

Nally, Revd James, PP Tarmonbarry, 172
Naomi, 71–3
'Night of the Big Wind', 23–4
Norfolk, 152

O'Beirne, Edwin, emigrant, **132**, 154
O'Beirne, Matilda, emigrant, **134**
O'Brien, Helen, historian, 177
O'Connell, Daniel, 42
O'Connor, Charles, landlord, 117
O'Donovan, John, antiquarian, 12, 53
O'Faolain, Nuala, writer, 180
O'Keefe, Catherine, emigrant, 144

Pakenham Mahon, Grace Catherine, 87–9, 164
Pakenham Mahon, Henry Sandford, 89, 98, 111, 114, 118, 131, 134, 137, 147, 160–1
Pakenham Mahon, Nicholas Hales, 163
Pakenham Mahon, Olive Hales, 1–2, 18, 163, 169, **180**, **182**

Pakenham Mahon, William Stuart Hales, 163, 169, 182
Pakenham, Revd, Dean of St Patricks, 130
Parks, William, tenant farmer, 40
Petrie, George, antiquarian, 171–2
Phytopthora infestans (potato blight), 34, 41, 133
Pope Pius IX, 101
post-Famine improvement, 157–8
Prince Albert, 101

Quebec, 67–8, 70, 137
Queen Victoria, 101
Queen's County, 149

relief committees (*panel*), 99
Reynolds, Albert, former Taoiseach, 181
Ridgway, Christopher, historian, 3
Roberts, Thomas, sub-agent, 90, 117, 133, 160
Robinson, J.&W., shipping agents, 67, 76
Robinson, John, bailiff, 70, 115, 125
Robinson, Mary, former President of Ireland, 179, **184**
Roe, William, estate solicitor, 155
Routh, Randolph, chair of Relief Commission, 101
Royal Irish Academy, 35

Saunders family, 70
Scally, Robert, historian, 175
secret societies (*panel*), 56
Shanley, Terence, MD, 27
Society of Friends (Quakers), 160
Southampton, 86
Steward & Kincaid, land agents, 152
Stokes, Robert, tenant farmer, 34
Strokestown Park, House, **xvi**, 1–4, **8**, **9**, **10**, **12**, 87, 179–87, **181**
Strokestown Loan Fund, 26–7
Strokestown Workhouse, **146**

Tarmonbarry, 23, 27
Tighe, Daniel (Tye), 74
Tipperary, county, 29
Tye, Mary, daughter of Daniel, **77**

Virginius, 71–3

Wakefield, Edward, 26–7
Wallace, Patrick, tenant, 44
Walpole, George, middleman, 116–17, 125, 128
Weld, Issac, 20
Woodham Smith, Cecil, 26